MOTOR

JL'

HUTTON PRESS
1998

Published by the Hutton Press Ltd.
130 Canada Drive, Cherry Burton, Beverley
East Yorkshire HU17 7SB

Printed by
Burstwick Print & Publicity Services
13a Anlaby Road, Hull, HU1 2PJ

ISBN 1 872167 94 2

(Front Cover)
The "GAUL" in her B.U.T. livery. Photo courtesy The Guardian newspaper.

(Front Cover)
The Bridge of the "GAUL", in her final resting place. Note the bridge windows intact.
Also visible is the builder's plate. Photo courtesy Anglia Television Ltd.

(Back Cover)
The Author, John Nicklin, at Grimsby Fish Dock. Photo courtesy of the Grimsby
Evening Telegraph.

1490

CONTENTS

FOREWORD

It is now twenty-four years since the Hull trawler "Gaul" sank with the loss of her thirty-six man crew in February 1974. At the time there was disbelief in Hull and elsewhere that a modern factory freezer could founder in a heavy sea without so much as a May-Day signal being sent.

This disbelief manifested itself in the emergence of a variety of theories as to the reasons for her loss. The most probable of these was that she was spying on the Russian fleet, had been boarded by her Navy and that the crew had been imprisoned in Soviet Russia. The first official acknowledgement of the use of Royal Naval personnel on Hull trawlers came in an answer to my Parliamentary Questions in 1974. They then admitted that it was only to gain seafaring experience on British trawlers. Only now have they revealed that some vessels were used to spy on Russian fleets - though this was denied at the time, with a further specific denial that the "Gaul" was involved. The full truth has so far been difficult to establish.

Over the years Hull has suffered many trawler losses, borne stoically by the families of the crews. But none has caused the same controversy as the loss of the "Gaul". Nor has the official explanation done much to allay the suspicions of the relatives of her crew. This has been the subject of much media attention, culminating in the discovery of her wreck by Anglia Television in a programme broadcast on Channel Four in 1997.

It is for these reasons that the Government has authorised a full underwater survey of the wreck to be undertaken in the Summer of 1998. Until the results of this survey are known, it is hoped that this present book by retired Skipper John Nicklin will go at least part of the way to explaining the circumstances surrounding the loss of the "Gaul".

May I take this opportunity to express my admiration for the way that the relatives have campaigned tirelessly to uncover facts which may only be verified upon publication of the survey.

Rt. Hon. John Prescott, MP.
House of Commons
April 1998.

ACKNOWLEDGEMENTS

The author wishes to acknowledge the co-operation given by the Marine Safety Agency in granting permission to quote from the National Maritime Institute's Report into the stability of the GAUL in a seaway.

Mrs Sonya De Marco Page at the Marine Information Centre, Marine Safety Agency for her help in research which went far beyond the call of duty. I found her to be everything a Civil Servant should be.

The Royal Institute of Naval Architects for permission to reproduce illustrations from Dr. A. Morrall's paper "The Gaul Disaster: An Investigation into the Loss of a Large Stern Trawler".

Kerry Meal of the Suffolk Records Office for help in providing relevant photographs and suggesting lines of research.

Peter Hansford, Brooke Marine Archivist, for providing archive material.

Skippers J. Williams, E. Suddaby and T. Thresh of Hull for photographs.

Norman Fenton and Anglia Television Ltd., for the underwater photographs of the GAUL.

Sir Barry Sheen Q.C. for photograph.

And finally my Publisher who knocked the manuscript into a state fit to go to the printer.

Without your help this book could never have been written and I am grateful to all of you.

John Nicklin
Cleethorpes
February 1998

Map of the "GAUL's" final voyage.

INTRODUCTION

Trawling is a dangerous game. A game where men pitted their wits against nature on some of the most desolate and violent expanses of water on the planet to reap the harvest of the seas. An occupation where the workforce suffered a greater loss of life and limb, and created more widows and orphans than any other. An industry which, between 1946 and 1975, lost over a hundred and twenty large trawlers through one cause or another, many of them with 'all hands'.

Some of these lost vessels were able to send out distress calls on the radio, and it was possible to establish the cause of the loss. Others, like the 600 ton Hull trawler ST ROMANUS, H 223, and her 20 man crew simply vanished without trace on or about 11th January 1968, and we will never know what happened to them.

Generally, whenever a trawler was lost, the local press at the ship's home port would print the details on the front page and perhaps an editorial on safety at sea. In those cases where there was heavy loss of life, the event might justify a paragraph or two in the national press, and a news flash on local radio and television. The Superintendent of the local branch of the Royal National Mission to Deep Sea Fishermen would go round and distribute his cargo of sympathy, and a memorial service would be held in the fishermen's chapel. The trawler owner would check his ship was adequately insured and consider the unlikely possibility of a claim for negligence being made against him. Then more news-worthy events would push the loss from the media, and it would be forgotten, except by relatives and dependants of the crew, who would retire with their grief behind closed doors away from public view, to be consoled by their own kind.

From the publicity angle, the loss of the GAUL was different to the usual run of trawler losses. A large, modern factory trawler, fishing on a bank in close proximity with over a dozen other similar ships with which she was in daily visual and radio contact, fitted with state of the art radio communication equipment, and loaded with the latest in life saving appliances and navigational aids, simply vanished from the sight of man, together with her 36 man crew. No distress call was sent or received, and no wreckage or oil slick was found. She simply disappeared, and an intensive air search by RAF Nimrods and Norwegian Airforce planes, Royal Navy and Norwegian Navy vessels, and dozens of trawlers and merchant ships in the area, found nothing. She was only about 200 miles from an area where the Soviet fleet had bases, and at the time she was lost the Western powers were holding a naval exercise less than 200 miles away to the southward. No doubt Russian intelligence vessels would be monitoring the proceedings. There were all the elements of a good news story, and even as long after the loss as October 1996, over 20 years after the event, television was still screening 'Spy Ship' documentaries claiming to show 'new evidence'.

A Formal Investigation into the circumstances of the loss was held by the Department of Trade at the City Hall, Hull, which found that GAUL capsized and foundered due to being overwhelmed by a succession of heavy seas, probably while she was coming round from before the wind to head to wind.

Despite the inquiry findings rumours began to circulate. It was claimed that GAUL was engaged in spying activities, and had been captured by the Russians and was being concealed in a Russian port. There was talk of a cover up by the British and Norwegian Governments. This was stuff for the media. The national press went to town on it, and the BBC ran a 'Spy Ship' programme at prime time television. Relatives of the GAUL's crewmen clung to the theory that their men might still be alive in a Russian port, and proceedings were started charging the owners with negligence, and claiming compensation. It was claimed that the GAUL's wireless operator had been seen in a bar in South Africa some time after the reputed foundering. A self-styled 'marine investigator' attempted to raise funds to enable a party of volunteers to comb the desolate Arctic coasts to search for possible wreckage, and while a considerable sum of money was reported to have been raised, and many local fishermen were willing to join the search party, it never got off the ground. The intention of this book is to set out the facts concerning the loss of the GAUL. The author has had considerable experience trawling in the area the GAUL was last seen, and has commanded a factory trawler of similar design to the GAUL. He will use that experience, and the sight of documents not available at the time of the official inquiry, to conclude with suggestions of two possible causes for the loss, which were not considered, and which are at least as plausible as the official verdict. In fact, he will attempt to prove that the GAUL could not possibly have been lost in the manner the Court of Inquiry put forward as probable.

The book is dedicated, not only to the crew of the GAUL, but also to all those other brave trawlermen lost at sea, and to the families that mourned them. They gave their all, and we owe them a debt. We should never forget them.

CHAPTER 1

THE SHIP

At the time of her loss, the motor trawler GAUL H243 was one of the most modern vessels sailing from Hull. Originally built as RANGER CASTOR by Brooke Marine for Ranger Fishing Company of South Shields, she was one of four similar ships. The contract for her was signed on 7th August 1969, she was launched on 6th December 1971, and delivered to her owners on 3rd August 1972. On 15th October 1973 she was sold to British United Trawlers and moved to Hull where she was re-registered as H243, and renamed GAUL. Her three sisters were the RANGER CADMUS, RANGER CALLIOPE and the RANGER CALLISTO. These ships were also purchased by B.U.T and registered at Hull, and renamed ARAB, KELT and KURD respectively.

She was a single screw factory stern trawler, designed to operate in the North and South Atlantic, and the Arctic, and to fillet and freeze her catch at sea. She was 1106.29 gross tons, 410.54 net tons, and at her designed draught of 15 feet 9 inches gave a load displacement of 1,851 tons. Her principal dimensions were as follows:

Length between perpendiculars. 186.5 feet
Length overall. 216.75 feet
Breadth. 40.0 feet
Depth to the trawl deck. 25.5 feet
Depth to the main deck. 17.5 feet

She was of all welded steel construction, and was built to Lloyds Register of Shipping Classification * 100 A1 (stern trawler), Class * LMC for her machinery, and Ice Class 3 for her hull. The ship had a raked keel, the rake being 2 feet by the stern, and she was fitted with port and starboard bilge keels extending for 58 feet amidships.

She was a two decker, the upper deck being the weather deck from which the trawl gear was worked, and below this weather deck was the factory deck.

Above the weather deck, a forecastle extended aft from the bows about half the length of the ship, the sides of which were continued aft for another 50 feet, and then cut down to form bulwarks 3.28 feet high which ran to the after end of the vessel. The engine casing, a CO_2 room, and a net store were situated on the port side of the weather deck, and there was a small vent compartment on the starboard side.

At the stern, the after end of the trawl deck (weather deck) the middle part of the deck was sloped down to form a ramp 20 feet long and 13 feet wide which ran from deck level to the water line at the stern. The purpose of this ramp was to facilitate the operation of hauling and shooting the trawl. The lower end of the ramp was open to the sea, and at the deck end two half doors, 3.5 feet high, were fitted which when closed helped to prevent seas coming aboard up the ramp. Just fore side of these doors were two flush hatches in the trawl deck which allowed the fish to be emptied on to a chute for conveyance to the factory deck for processing. These hatches could be opened and closed either hydraulically or manually, and when closed were made watertight by rubber seals.

Rectangular freeing ports were cut in the bulwarks on each side along the entire length of the trawl deck, clear of the deck houses. These ports were 3 feet long and 0.75 feet high, and there were 13 ports on the starboard side, and 10 on the port side. The effective area of these ports was reduced by them being fitted with vertical bars. A well was formed on the trawl deck by bobbin rails, 22 inches high, which was 80 feet long and 21 feet wide at the fore end, tapering to 13 feet wide at the after end. Within this well was a clear area for unshipping machinery, and at the fore end, an enclosed space called the net arena.

The interior of the vessel was divided into compartments by watertight bulkheads. The fore peak bulkhead extended to the weather deck, but all the others finished at the factory deck to allow continuous working space the full length of the deck. Starting from the fore end, there was the fore peak tank used for water ballast, oil fuel deep tank, fish hold, fish meal hold, engine room, port, starboard and centre (tunnel) oil fuel tanks, and liver oil tank. A double bottom ran from the oil fuel deep tank to the after end of the engine room, which was divided into oil and ballast water compartments.

The steering gear compartment was on the centre line on the after end of the factory deck. Abreast of this, on the starboard side and in line from aft, was a net store, chill water plants and a liver plant. On the port side, again starting from the after end, was an engineers' store, a converter room, an engineers' workshop, and the engine casing.

Fore side of the steering gear were fish chutes leading to the compartments in which the fish was processed. These compartments ran the full width of the deck as far as frame 58.

From frame 58 to frame 80 was the crew accommodation, and from frame 80 to frame 92 was the refrigerating machinery compartment and the anchor chain locker. A store room ran from this point to the stem.

 Access to the forecastle was by means of a door on the port side of the trawl deck just fore side the trawl winch. A small deckhouse on the forecastle deck held the master's and officers' accommodation, and above this, on the bridge deck, was the navigating bridge, chart room and radio room. At the fore end of the forecastle deck was a hatch providing access to the store in the forecastle, and there was another hatch positioned abaft the breakwater giving access to the fish hold.

The main engine of the vessel was a 16 cylinder English Electric Type 16 RK3M 4 Stroke Cycle Single Acting diesel engine rated at 2600 brake horse power at 750 revolutions per minute. This engine drove a single Escher-Wyss controllable pitch propeller through a reduction gearbox. It also drove a 300 Kilowatt D.C electric generator. Engine power gave the ship a maximum speed of 13.5 knots. The D.C generator powered the lighting and the steering gear, and could also be used as a motor in an emergency, giving 375 shaft horsepower which would propel the ship at 3.5 knots.

The VP propeller was controlled from the bridge, with duplicate controls in the engine room. Steering gear comprised a Donkin electro - hydraulic motor driving a swivel Kort nozzle.

Navigation equipment comprised gyro and magnetic compasses, automatic steering, two radar sets, Decca navigator, direction finder, and Loran.

Radio communications equipment fitted on the GAUL comprised a Redifon G341B mains powered transmitter, capable of worldwide transmission on radio telegraphy, or on radiotelephony on high or medium frequencies; a Redifon GR 497 radio telephone with a range of 300 miles, capable of battery operation; a Redifon GR 670 VHF radio telephone with a range of between 20 and 30 miles; two emergency lifeboat transmitters capable of transmitting speech only on 2182 KHz, and an automatic distress signal generating device fitted to the radio telephone transmitter.

The lifesaving appliances on board the GAUL were sufficient for 50 persons. She had one glass reinforced plastic Class C lifeboat; six inflatable liferafts, four of which provided for 25 persons each and two for four persons each; 51 lifejackets, 4 lifebuoys, and a line throwing apparatus.

Fire fighting appliances positioned around the vessel included fire pumps, hoses, extinguishers, breathing apparatus, a fire axe and safety lamp, carbon dioxide smothering arrangements to machinery and cargo spaces, an emergency fire pump, and a Minerva smoke/heat detection unit.

The above text is a very accurate description of the GAUL and her equipment drawn up from her Certificates, and from the minutes of the Official Enquiry into the circumstances of her loss. If later, when we have all the facts, we are going to offer intelligent theories on how the loss occurred, it is essential that we establish right at the onset that the GAUL was a well found ship, built to the highest Lloyds specifications for her class, and equipped so as to meet all Department of Trade and IMCO safety recommendations. One of the mysteries we have to solve is why, although the weather was very bad at the time she vanished, other ships in the same area, some smaller and possibly less well equipped, survived. She shouldn't have been lost, but she was.

Aerial view of the shipyard of Brooke Marine Ltd., Lowestoft, September 1973. From the Brooke Marine Archives.

Above: The "Ranger Cadmus", the first of the four "C" class trawlers built for the Ranger Fishing Company at North Shields, pictured here on her sea trials. She became part of the B.U.T. fleet in 1973 and was re-named the "Arab" (H 238). Photo courtesy Ford Jenkins and Suffolk Record Office.

Below: The second of the "C" class trawlers, the "Ranger Calliope" on her sea trials. Bought by B.U.T. in 1973 she was re-named the "Kelt" (H 240). Photo courtesy Ford Jenkins and Suffolk Record Office.

The third of the "C" class trawlers, the "Ranger Callisto", at her launch at the Brooke Marine Yard in June 1971. Bought by B.U.T. in 1973 she was re-named the "Kurd" (H 242). Photo courtesy Ford Jenkins and Suffolk Record Office.

The "Ranger Callisto" on her sea trials. Photo courtesy Suffolk Record Office.

Form of Service

to be held at the

Launching Ceremony of

Ranger Castor

Stern Fishing Freezer Trawler

for Ranger Fishing Company Ltd.

on Monday, 6th December

1971

from the
Shipyard of Brooke Marine Limited
Lowestoft

NAMING CEREMONY
BY MRS. J. BAYLEY

The launching ceremony of the "Ranger Castor" (the "GAUL"), the fourth of the "C" class trawlers, at the Brooke Marine Yard on 6th Dcember 1971. From the Brooke Marine achives.

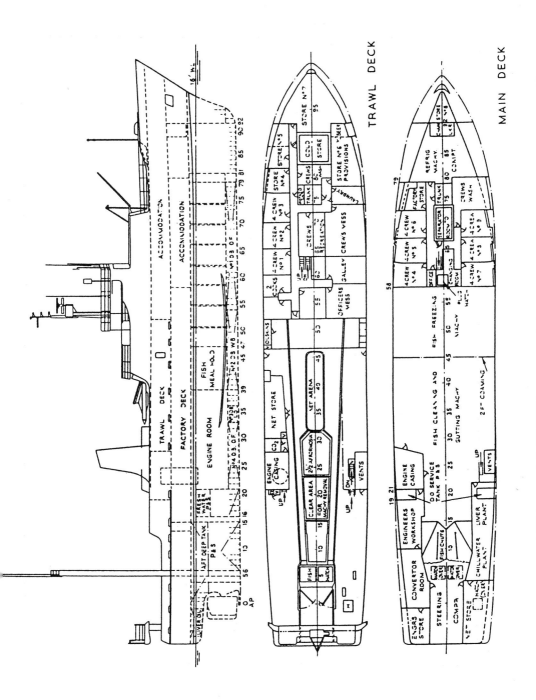

Plan of the "Ranger Castor" (the "GAUL"). Courtesy the Royal Institute of Naval Architects.

Above: The "Ranger Castor" (SN 18) pictured in 1972. Photo courtesy the National Fishing Heritage Centre, Grimsby.

One of the few surviving photographs of the "GAUL" when re-named. She was bought by B.U.T. in October 1973. Photo courtesy The Guardian newspaper.

Lloyd's Register of Shipping

Certificate of Class

We hereby certify that the........................ Motor Stern Trawler.
.... "RANGER CASTOR" now named "GAUL".

Lloyd's Register No...7126724......................... REGISTERED TONNAGES
Built by...Brooke Marine Ltd................. Gross .....1106.29.....................
.... Net ....410.54.....................
at ....Lowestoft.................................. MOULDED DIMENSIONS
date ....July, 1972........................... .Length ...186'............6"..............
                                          Breadth   40'   0"

having been built in accordance with the Rules and Regulations under the Special
Survey of the Society's Surveyors and reported by them on........28/7/72.....................
to be in a fit and efficient condition, has been assigned the class of....✠100A1.............
"Stern Trawler" Ice Class 3...

In the Register Book subject to continued compliance with the requirements of the
Society's Rules and Regulations.

Chairman

Secretary

Date of issue..22nd February, 1974.
71, Fenchurch Street, London, EC3M 4BS

C. 1000

The "GAUL's" Lloyd's Certificate, February 1974.

19

CHAPTER 2

THE LAST VOYAGE

The GAUL sailed from Hull shortly after 06.00 on the 22nd January 1974, under the command of Skipper Peter Nellist on her final voyage.

Skipper Nellist was a relief skipper making his first voyage on the GAUL. He was a very experienced trawlerman, having held a Skipper's Certificate for over 15 years. In 1965 he had commanded four large side trawlers, and between October 1967 and April 1971 he commanded CASSIO on four occasions.

He became the permanent Skipper of ORSINO in February 1973, and held this position until he was transferred to the GAUL in January 1974. He was regarded by the Company as a conscientious and reliable skipper.

Shortly before the GAUL sailed Skipper Nellist and her crew of 33 hands joined her, and just prior to sailing, Mr. G. Northard, a shipping master employed by the vessel's owners, assisted by the Mate, Mr. George Petty, made a rough check to ensure that all the crew were on board, and that all visitors to the ship had disembarked. However, shortly after leaving Hull a stowaway, Mr John Heywood, was found on board, and because he was an experienced fisherman, and wanted a job, the Skipper signed him on the Articles as a general purpose hand. Later that same day, the GAUL stopped off Bridlington to collect another crewman, Mr. W. Tracey, who was signed on as a spare hand.

Immediately after Mr. Tracey had boarded, the GAUL resumed her passage towards the fishing grounds off the Norwegian coast. En route, Mr. Petty became ill, and Skipper Nellist decided to go into port to obtain medical assistance. She arrived at Lodigen on the 26th January, and it was found that Mr. Petty was suffering from a rupture, and was medically unfit to continue the fishing voyage. Accordingly, he was put ashore for conveyance back to Hull.

The owners were advised of the Mate's incapacity, and it was arranged that a relief mate would be flown out to Tromso. GAUL left Lodigen at 1600 hours on the 27th and proceeded to Tromso where Mr.M.E.Spurgeon joined her as the replacement Mate. She sailed from Tromso at 02.30 on the 28th January and started fishing the next day in position 71 degrees 50 minutes North, 29 degrees 10 minutes East. At this time there were 36 men, including the Skipper, on board.

For the next nine days the GAUL continued fishing in the vicinity of North Cape Bank among a number of other trawlers. Periodically she was sighted by other vessels working in the area. She was in frequent radio contact with them, and reported her position to her owners daily on the Freezers Schedule. The last report made by her was at 10.00 7th February, when she gave her position as 72 degrees 15 minutes North, 24 degrees 50 minutes East. That same day the GAUL made a radio link call to the owner's office to report a fault on the Sperry auto-pilot. The inference from this is that she was experiencing some trouble with her steering, which may, or may not, have been a contributory cause of her loss.

On the following morning, the 8th February, the GAUL was seen by Mr. Bill Brayshaw, the Mate of SWANELLA. At that time, he was talking on the VHF to Maurice Spurgeon, Mate of the GAUL. The GAUL passed SWANELLA, steaming in a westerly direction, about a mile off her starboard beam. Mr Brayshaw later told the Inquiry that at the time the GAUL and SWANELLA passed each other, GAUL appeared fit in every respect to cope with the prevailing weather conditions. At 10.45 that morning SWANELLA was heading into the wind on a course of 110 degrees, and the echo of GAUL was seen by Mr. Brayshaw about 6 miles astern. That was the last reported sighting of the GAUL.

At 09.30 that morning GAUL's report on the office schedule, via PICT was "Laid and dodging near North Cape Bank." At 10.30 she reported to ORSINO on the Skipper's Freezer Schedule. Between 11.06 and 11.09 two private telegrams were sent by GAUL by radio though Wick Radio. These were the last known radio messages from her. From that moment she was never seen or heard of again.

At the Official Inquiry, Skipper Madden of the KELT was questioned about Skipper Nellist.

"Was he (Nellist) the sort of man you would expect to keep quiet for a period or stick to the arrangements you had?"

Skipper Madden replied "He would stick to the Sched. It was not Pete to keep off the Scheds. He was a man who would keep to the book".

The fact that the GAUL did not report on the 16.30 Skipper's Schedule that day gave the other vessels no cause for alarm because at the 10.30 Schedule that day there were reports from 17 freezer trawlers, but at 16.30 only 8 trawlers reported to ORSINO. Thus there was nothing unusual at that time to put Skipper Spencer of ORSINO on enquiry.

All the foregoing is indisputable fact, and from the evidence it seems likely that whatever happened to the GAUL did so between 11.09, when she was in radio contact with Wick Radio, and 16.30 when she failed to report on the Schedule on 8th February 1974, a period when the weather was at its worst.

Three witnesses gave evidence to the Enquiry that they had heard on their private radios distress messages they believed had come from the GAUL on Saturday, 9th February, but the Court heard evidence from Mr.G.H. Sturge, Assistant Head of the Engineering Information Department of the B.B.C. that while signals transmitted on either 500 KHz or 2182 KHz (the distress frequencies) could have been received in the U.K. on a suitable receiver and aerial system, it was not possible for a listener tuned in to Radio Humberside on either medium wave or V.H.F. to have received such signals. The Court was satisfied that the witnesses who thought they heard such signals were mistaken. There was some very slight hearsay evidence that the GAUL was still afloat and was in a foreign port . That theory was totally unsupported by any evidence acceptable to the Court, and was rejected.

Three months later, on the 8th May, Mr. Arnt Olsen, the Skipper of the

Norwegian vessel M.V. ROVER, while engaged in small whale fishing in the Barents Sea, picked up a lifebuoy marked "GAUL HULL" in a position 71 degrees 25 minutes North, 28 degrees 15 minutes East. It was identified as coming from the GAUL by Mr Harold Hinchcliffe, a painter employed by Hull Trawlers Supplies Company Ltd., who had painted and lettered the lifebuoy for the GAUL. Up to the date of the Inquiry, that lifebuoy was the only trace of the GAUL that was found.

The following are a series of photographs of features of the four "C" class trawlers from the Brooke Marine archives.

The factory deck looking aft showing the Baader processing machines.

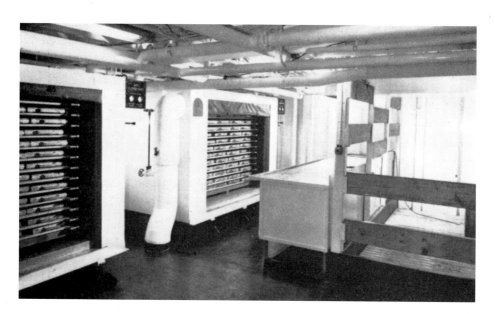

Above: The APV Clarke-built horizontal freezers.

Below: The eight-cylinder compound refrigerating compressors.

Above: The wheelhouse instruments include Decca radar, Elac and Marconi-Koden echo sounders, fischlupe and Superlodar sonar.

The Skipper's day room.

24

Left: The crew's mess room.

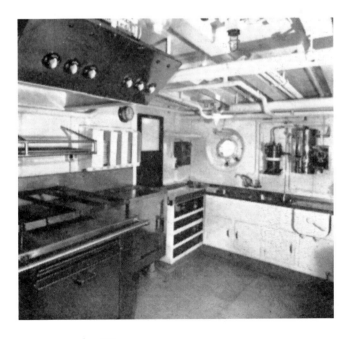

Right: The well-fitted galley situated between the crew's and the officers' mess.

Above: The sixteen cylinder English Electric diesel engine.

Below: Part of the Redifon equipment in the radio room.

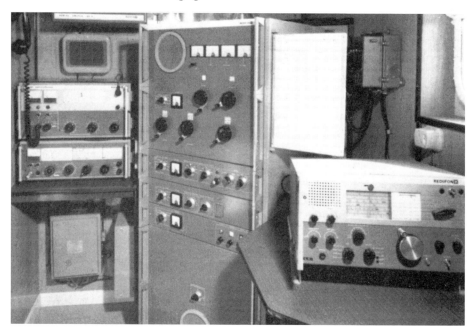

CHAPTER 3

THE WEATHER

In investigating the causes of any ship lost at sea, it is essential to establish wind and sea conditions in the area at the time of the loss. In the case of the loss of the GAUL this is not difficult.

There were over a dozen trawlers working in the vicinity of North Cape Bank on the morning of 8th February, and the Skippers and Mates of these ships are in general agreement that on that morning the wind was increasing in force, with a corresponding effect upon the sea. The 10.30 Skipper Freezer Schedule received aboard the ORSINO lists 12 trawlers in that area that were laid and dodging because of bad weather.

Mr. William Brayshaw, Mate of SWANELLA, estimated weather conditions at about 09.00 as follows: "pretty bad - Force 7 or 8 at the time. From time to time there were snow squalls which reduced visibility to nil. Between the squalls visibility was several miles." Continuing his evidence, he went on to state "By 11.00 the wind had increased to Force 9 or even 10, but this is guess work again." He was asked "What sort of seas were you encountering?", to which he replied "these were pretty huge seas." There were three particularly large waves which knocked SWANELLA off course, the first of which caused him to put the wheel hard over to port to get the ship back head to wind. One very large wave hit the port corner of the bridge, causing considerable damage by twisting an engineers' derrick round the front of the bridge. Replying to the question "Have you ever experienced seas like that before?" he said "yes, not that trip. I have only seen it another once." Skipper Richard Spencer of ORSINO also estimated that the wind was Force 7 or 8 at about 10.30 and added: "At times there were some very high seas running, but only for short spaces of time, and then it would ease off a bit. There were times when the seas were very high, as high as the bridge of the ship I was in command of."

Mr. Ernest McCoid, Mate of PICT, gave evidence that the PICT was in the same area off the North Cape as GAUL. The PICT was fishing until 02.00 on Friday 8th February when the weather deteriorated so rapidly that the trawl was pulled away and all the fishing gear was lost. At about 15.00 on Saturday 9th when dodging head to wind PICT met a terrific sea which stopped the ship altogether and caused considerable damage to the plating on the front of the bridge.

There was some suggestion at the Inquiry that the evidence of eye-witnesses as to the strength of the wind, and the height of the seas 'may have been coloured by the fact that they were viewing the situation from a small ship' (reports of structural damage to several ships in the area were certainly not 'coloured'), and 'expert' technical evidence was called for from Mr. Lawrence Draper, a member of the staff of the Institute of Oceanographic Sciences. He said that no wave measurements were available for the area for February, 1974, but gave his expert opinion on the probable height of the waves derived from a study of the reports of wind conditions. He had formed the opinion that the wind had reached Force 9 (45 knots) by 06.00 and remained at that force until noon. He estimated that the significant wave height to be 22 feet at 10.30 on the 8th February, and 25 feet at 16.30. He further estimated that the significant period (of the waves) to be 11.3 seconds at 10.30 and 12 seconds at 16.30. The length of a wave can be calculated from its period, and the mentioned significant periods indicate waves much longer than those described by eye-witnesses. 'Significant wave height' is defined as the average height of the highest one-third of all the waves, and 'significant period' means the average period of those same waves. It is important to realise that these periods only relate to the longest one-third of all waves, and there is substantial and convincing evidence that many waves were shorter and steeper than this evidence suggests. In the course of his evidence Mr. Draper explained that in any known sea conditions there is a finite and calculable chance that a wave or waves will be higher than the most probable value. For example, when the significant height is 22 feet and the most probable value of the height of the highest wave in three hours is 43 feet, there is a 10 per cent chance that a wave of 49 feet will occur. He made it clear that one wave formation could overtake another slower wave formation and as one crest tries to overtake another, a larger wave is formed as they get nearer coincidence.

The Court drew Mr. Draper's attention to the evidence of the Mate of the SWANELLA quoted above and asked him:

"What are the prospects of getting three waves of about 48 feet, one rapidly after another?"

He replied "When the wave components are getting into phase you will have gradually increasing wave heights. When they are getting out of phase the height will decline. It is not uncommon to have two, three, or even four wave troughs bigger than the general run of waves - this depends on the general run of waves and the relative speed of the components.

He stressed that his estimate of wave height was dependent on the accuracy of the estimated wind speed of 45 knots. If the wind was blowing at Force 10 (51 knots) for several hours a wave of over 50 feet could be experienced.

From the evidence of eye-witnesses, and the scientific evidence, we can safely conclude that the sea was very rough, and that it is very likely that some exceptionally high waves were present from time to time on North Cape Bank on the 8th of February. Whether or not the GAUL could survive such conditions, bearing in mind that over a dozen ships in the area did survive, we reserve judgement until later when we have studied the vessel's stability data.

Regular Skipper, 'Ernest Suddaby described the "GAUL" as the best ship he ever sailed on.

Skipper Peter Nellist who sailed with the "GAUL" on her fateful voyage on 22nd January 1974.

Below: Graham Hellyer, Managing Director of B.U.T. (far right), with his brother Mark Hellyer (second right), Tom Boyd (left) and J.R. Cobley, Vice President of the British Trawler Federation (second left). Photo courtesy of Arthur Credland, Hull's Town Dock Museum.

CHAPTER 4

THE SHIP REPORTING PROCEDURE

The Committee of Inquiry into Trawler Safety chaired by Admiral Sir Deric Holland-Martin made recommendations for a system of position reporting by fishing vessels at sea, and the action management ashore should take when a vessel failed to report. The owners of the GAUL had put in place a reporting system that was even better than that recommended by Holland-Martin.

Company Standing Orders to Skippers required every Skipper to report his position, fishing results and other relevant information to a control ship each day. This report was made in Company code, and the control ship always sent this coded information to a coast radio station for transmission to the Company office, where it was usually received between 10.00 and noon.

As soon as this message from the control ship had been decoded the information contained in it was entered in the office freezer schedule. Communications received outside office hours and at weekends were handled by four duty officers who worked a rota so that no period was uncovered. The duty officer's job was to decode any messages received in the evenings or weekends, and enter the information in the freezer schedule. He also had a duty to inform the trawler manager on duty of any information requiring action to be taken or of any abnormal fishing or position report. It was general practice for the duty officer to get in touch with the duty trawler manager at 18.00 on Saturdays and Sundays.

On that fateful weekend Mr. David Close, an assistant cashier employed by the Company, was the duty officer, a position he had filled in his turn for the previous ten years. As stated above, it was his duty to decode any telegrams received, and to compile the schedule report for Friday night and Saturday morning. On Saturday 9th February the morning schedule came in about 11.30. It was timed 09.30 and had been sent by the trawler PICT. On decoding the message, Mr. Close noticed that the GAUL was missing from the list of freezers. This omission gave him no cause for concern at the time because sometimes trawlers sent messages independent of the control ship, and when a ship did send its own report there could be a delay on account of it being sent through a different coast station. Mr. Close stated that a report from the GAUL could have arrived later in the afternoon, and that on occasions he had received messages up to four or five o'clock.

When the schedule report arrived at 11.30 the duty trawler manager had already left the office, but before leaving he had told Mr. Close that he would telephone Mr. Close at about 6 o'clock that evening. This was contrary to usual practice, it being customary for the duty officer to contact the trawler manager.

Mr. Close stayed at the office until noon when he closed down the telex, transferred all incoming calls to his home number, then went home. Late that afternoon he rang the Post Office to see if there were any further telegrams, just in case there was one from the GAUL. He stayed at home for the rest of the day but did not receive the expected telephone call from the duty trawler manager.

On Sunday morning 10th February, Mr. Close phoned the telegrams office at Leeds and Bradford and took messages in the Fleet Code. These were all decoded by 11.00 and they contained no reference to GAUL. His first action was to ring Mr. Sabberton, the Superintendent Engineer, to enquire if he had received any message from the GAUL regarding a mechanical breakdown. The answer was "No". He then tried, without success, to get in touch with the duty trawler manager. By this time there had been no sched report from the GAUL since the previous Friday and he was becoming concerned. On his own initiative at 11.55 he sent out a SPY message via Bradford and Wick Radio.

A SPY message says "Why have you not reported your position as per Company Standard Instructions."

At about 13.30 Mr. Close spoke to the duty manager on the phone, told him that GAUL had not reported, and that he had sent out a SPY message.

It was usual practice for an employee of the U.K. Trawlers Mutual Insurance Company to telephone all trawler owners at about noon each day to establish whether all the ships had made their daily reports. Mr. Raymond Brookes, personal assistant to the managing director of the insurance company, spoke to Mr. Close on the telephone at 14.00 that Sunday afternoon and learned that the GAUL had not reported and that a SPY message had been sent, to which a reply was expected late that afternoon. When there was no reply from GAUL Mr. Close again contacted Mr. Brookes, and it was decided to put through a link call to ORSINO. When difficulties arose over making radio contact with ORSINO, Mr. Brookes decided to telephone Mr. Arne Isachsen, the insurance company's agent in Tromso. The agent was told of GAUL's failure to report and he promised to speak to Hammerfest Radio to have enquiries made about the position of the GAUL. Hammerfest Radio is a coast station that handles vessels' wireless communications. Mr. Isachsen telephoned Mr. Brookes again later that evening and said that he would alert vessels fishing off the Norwegian coast, and that HMS MOHAWK had been alerted.

By 09.00 on Monday 11th February, there was still no news of the GAUL, and as a result, Mr. Brookes spoke to Captain Habesch, a nautical assistant employed by the insurance company, and it was decided to put out a GZWT message. GZWT is the collective call sign for all vessels insured by U.K. Trawlers Insurance Company. At 09.25 the following message was sent via Wick Radio:

"To all vessels fishing North Bank Norway - all vessels please report any contact with GAUL last reported fishing on North Bank. Nil reports not required."

Shortly afterwards a call was put through to the Tromso agent asking for further information to which the reply was that there was still no news of GAUL, and that MOHAWK and other ships had been alerted.

At 12.35 a telephone call from Norway to Captain Habesch informed him that the Rescue Co-ordination Centre at Bodo, Norway, had been put on full alert and they required a description of the GAUL. Shortly after 13.00 Captain Habesch telephoned other Hull trawler owners and asked for their assistance in joining in a search for the GAUL. All owners agreed to co-operate, and Boyd Line, Marr and Hamling, who had ships in the area, sent messages to their ships at sea asking for information. At the same time a general message was sent out by the insurers to all ships insured with U.K. Mutual asking for an urgent report of any contact with GAUL.

At 14.10 Captain Habesch spoke to a Mr. Malcolm Jennings at the Hull office of the M.A.F.F. and asked if there was any possibility of an air search by UK based aircraft. Mr. Jennings telephoned the coastguards at Flamborough and spoke to Mr. Hardcastle, the duty officer, and told him of the situation, that the Norwegian authorities were on full alert, and that British trawlers and naval vessels were searching the area. He also told him there was a specific request to the coastguard that if possible a UK air search should be laid on, and that the Norwegian authorities had already started an air search.

Wick Radio considered that because of the distance involved it would be better for a PAN broadcast to be made by Vardo Radio than by Wick, and requested this.

The above is a complete description of the reporting procedures, and a chronological record of events established by the Inquiry. There was no position report from GAUL after the morning of Friday 8th of February, and a full air and sea search were not started until Monday 11th February. There seems no doubt that if a duty trawler manager had been able to be contacted, or had not omitted to make a telephone call, this search would have been started earlier. Up to date, this was the only evidence of possible negligence - a duty officer not available when he should have been - brought out by the Inquiry, although the Court considered that this made no difference to the eventual outcome. "We know of no case where a search following a failure of a trawler to report her position saved any lives that would have otherwise been lost ...."

In all fairness to the management of British United Trawlers they made every effort to implement an efficient reporting system. An internal memorandum dated 28th August 1974 (about 6 months after the loss of GAUL) was sent out by Graham Hellyer, chairman and managing director of Hellyer Brothers Ltd. and managing director of British United Trawlers, to D.M.Oswald, A.P.Hudson and G.A.Hartley, trawler managers, which read :

"I am concerned at the number of times our vessels fail to report their positions in accordance with the Company's Instructions. Tabulated below are the names of Skippers and Vessels that SPY messages have had to be sent out to in the last six months. There follows a list of 35 offenders. The memorandum continues: Certain Skippers . . . . seem to have records for irresponsibility - on the other hand, many skippers would appear to report regularly unfailingly. If verbal reprimands by management do not ensure that Company Standing Orders are complied with, then management must take stronger disciplinary action."

In fact, ships had to report at 09.00 each day and this report was relayed to the office each morning. They also had to report to the control ship at 21.00 each day. If any ship should fail to report at either 09.00 or 21.00 then the control ship had to inform the office of this fact and give the last know position of the vessel. In cases when a vessel was fishing alone and not in contact with a control ship she must report to the office direct at 09.00 and 21.00.

A stern trawler in a heavy sea.

CHAPTER 5

THE SEARCH

As soon as it became established, on the afternoon of Monday 11 February, that there were no radio signals from the GAUL a massive search operation was started by the Norwegian Authorities, the Royal Navy, and the Royal Air Force. This operation was in conjunction with a search being mounted by 23 trawlers already in the area.

Between the 11th and 15th February 177,000 square miles of sea were thoroughly searched. The Norwegians flew 13 sorties with Orion long range patrol aircraft and four areas were searched by RAF Nimrods. A long stretch of the Norwegian coastline was combed by Sea King helicopters and coastguard cutters.

The sea search by ships was organised by Captain C.R.P.C. Branson, Commanding Officer H.M.S. HERMES. The HERMES was on passage south to the Lofoten Islands area to participate in a four day exercise with Norwegian forces arranged by the Commander Allied Naval Forces Northern Norway. At 22.36 on the 10th February the Commander ordered HERMES and HNOMS STAVANGER to proceed to conduct a search for the GAUL. Captain Branson considered that vessels involved in the search would require refuelling and ordered R.F.A. TIDEFLOW to proceed to the area. In addition to HERMES, MOHAWK, STAVANGER, and TIDEFLOW the Norwegian vessels TRONDHEIM, NORDKAPPE and SENJA took part.

The search was conducted in very bad weather conditions, the temperature of the water such that any person in the sea could have survived only for a short time. Despite the bad weather, the search was so intensive that if there had been any wreckage afloat in the area searched it would almost certainly been found. The sea search was called off at 16.00 on Friday 15th February, and although after this, many vessels passed through the area, while flotsam from other vessels was seen and reported, no trace of wreckage from GAUL was discovered. The air search was continued by Nimrods and helicopters until the 22nd. The following messages received by the insurers at Hull fix the time the air search was terminated:

From Ministry of A. & F. from Bodo, Norway through Flamborough Coastguard.

21st February 1974. "At a meeting at 0730 today it was decided to make a last search with helicopter along the coastline in North Cape area to look for any small pieces of wreckage from GAUL. Helicopter airborne at 0912 and is still in the area searching."

0915 22 February 1974 From RHQ Flamborough.

"Following received from RCC Bodo at 1706 GMT: Air search with two helicopters has been carried out around the North Cape and in the fjords of Mageroeya today. Nothing has been found and the search has been called off. We have no intentions of recommence search. One UK Nimrod is carrying out search in Norwegian Sea but the aircraft has not been in contact with RCC Bodo."

Received from NRCC Pitreavie at 1740 GMT :

"Aircraft carried out search today and found nothing. Aircraft is now landed at Andoya Air Base and intends doing another sortie tomorrow in the area of Bear Island. Ends."

Up to that time, despite the intensive search, no trace of wreckage or oil was found. Then, on 8th May, three months after the GAUL disappeared, Mr. Arnt Olsen, Skipper of the motor vessel ROVER, while engaged in small whale fishing in the Barents Sea, found a lifebuoy marked 'GAUL HULL' in position 71 degrees 25 minutes North, 28 degrees 15 minutes East. This lifebuoy was positively identified as coming from the GAUL by Mr. Harold Hinchcliffe, a painter employed by Hull Trawlers Supply Company Ltd. who claimed to have painted the lettering on the buoy. Up to the date of the Official Inquiry started on 21st November 1974 that lifebuoy was the only trace of GAUL that had been found, and there was a suggestion made at the Inquiry that it had been 'planted'. When the lifebuoy was found by the ROVER it was taken on board and was not washed or cleaned. The Police Office in Vardo carefully packed it in plastic for shipping back to England. On arrival in the U.K. it was sent to Mr. Norman Hendey, a consultant on problems relating to marine biology. Initially, Mr Hendey formed the view that there was so little marine growth on the lifebuoy that it had not been long in the water. He also noted an absence of deep water plankton which suggested that it had never been far from shore, and had been floating in relatively shallow water for most of the time. This evidence is a contradiction of evidence relating to the position the the GAUL was presumed to have sunk. However, later in his evidence, Mr. Hendey explained that a material factor in the life of deep sea plankton flora is the incidence of light. He expressed the view that, bearing in mind the lack of solar illumination in latitudes so far north between February, when GAUL disappeared, and April when the lifebuoy was found, there was no reason to doubt that it had been in the water since early February.

Years after the date of the Inquiry, other traces of the GAUL were found.

An Internal Memo from Mr. D. Oswald to Mr. Graham Hellyer dated 2nd March 1977 advises that the outer case of a liferaft had been picked up by the Hull trawler MARBELLA in a position 72 degrees 03 minutes North, 25 degrees 04 minutes East, and had been identified by its markings as coming from GAUL.

About two years later, on 26th March 1979, the Norwegian trawler MAKKAUR picked up the outer cover of a 25 man liferaft in position 72 degrees 10 minutes North, 25 degrees 10 minutes East marked "BEAUFORT 2721 CoServiced 24/5/73 Ranger Fishing." These markings established it had belonged to GAUL.

From the evidence thrown up by the Inquiry so far, and the subsequent finding of the liferaft covers, while just how GAUL met her end is not clear, there seemed little doubt that she lay on the seabed in the North Cape Bank area.

CHAPTER 6

STABILITY OF GAUL AND THE INQUIRY FINDINGS

The later part of the evidence into the loss of the GAUL was concerned with her stability and her ability to cope with the weather conditions that existed in the vicinity of North Cape Bank at the time she was lost.

The Court questioned Skippers and Mates with previous experience of sailing in the GAUL or her sisters as to the sea keeping qualities of this class of vessel. Skipper Ernest Suddaby had been Skipper of GAUL for 11 months in 1973 and described her as the best ship he had ever been in. If we accept Skipper Suddaby's evidence, and there is no reason why we shouldn't, we must again ask the question "On the 8th and 9th February there were many other trawlers in the same area as GAUL and they were all able to ride out the storm. Why couldn't the GAUL ?"

An independent investigation into the safety of the GAUL as built was made by Y-ARD, Marine Consultants of Glasgow on behalf of the owners. This investigation examined the stability and seaworthiness characteristics of the ship in the condition of loading she was estimated to be in at the time of the disaster. Similar trials were also carried out by the Department of Trade. Both these investigations agreed that the initial and large - angle stability criteria advised by the Inter-governmental Consultative Organisation (IMCO) for trawlers was met with a big margin. This advice calls for a minimum value of metacentric height (GM) and minimum areas under the curve of statical stability at angles of heel of 30 and 40 degrees.

It was obvious that water could get on the trawl deck in bad weather, either up the ramp or over the bulwarks, and that this water would take some time to clear. Therefore investigations were made as to the effects of this water on stability. This water would affect the ship's seaworthiness in two ways. First of all, the weight of water on the ship at a position well above the centre of gravity would reduce the metacentric height (GM), and secondly there would be the free surface effect of this water on stability. Their calculations showed that if water was trapped between the bobbin rails only, though stability would be reduced, the ship would still maintain a positive metacentric height. However, if the level of water was above the bobbin rails, and extended the full width of the ship, the free surface effect would be so large that the metacentric height would become negative, and the ship would be initially unstable. These stability calculations were based on static considerations, and would represent the situation on board the ship for a very short time, and in reality, only instantaneously. This meant that the speed that water could be removed from the deck once it had come aboard was important, hence the freeing ports in the bulwarks were investigated. The area of these ports was found to be up to IMCO recommendations, but their effectiveness was reduced considerably by various obstructions in front of them. The calculated time to clear the deck of water outside the bobbin rails from 22 inches to 3 inches was 28 seconds if the freeing ports were fully effective, but if the effective area estimated by Y-ARD was used, the time would be 54.5 seconds for the port side, and 37.8 seconds for the starboard side. (Note: at a later date, after the official inquiry, other 'experts' made calculations that showed it would be impossible for GAUL to hold enough water on the trawl deck to render her to a condition from which she could not recover. We will look at this evidence later, but for now our interest is in the Inquiry findings.)

There was much discussion during the Inquiry as to whether water had been allowed to accumulate on the factory deck in sufficient quantity to affect stability. This could have occurred in two ways. Water may have entered from the deck through an open or imperfectly closed door. There is no evidence to suggest that this happened. (Nor is there any to suggest that it didn't). Secondly, flooding could have occurred through hoses being left running, and failure by those on board to notice the accumulating water. This does not seem reasonable because engine room staff would be passing though the factory deck while going to and from the engine room, and would have noticed it. But if water had been allowed to accumulate on this deck it would have contributed to loss of stability.

Damage to the ship below the waterline was considered. Calculations showed that the spacing of water-tight bulkheads was such that any one compartment could be flooded, or in some cases, two adjacent compartments, without the ship sinking or capsizing. If the fish hold and the spaces above were flooded however, the ship would be unstable. The Court decided that such flooding was not the cause of the loss because if the hull had been damaged so as to allow this to happen there would have been time for a distress message to have been transmitted.

Having considered all the above significant evidence we can follow the reasoning for the Court of Inquiry's findings. GAUL was equipped with radio transmitters which could transmit on medium and short waves. She had been 'on the air' to Wick at 11.06 on the morning of the 8th February, and had spoken to SWANELLA on the VHF that same morning. Had she sent out a distress message, or switched on her automatic alarm equipment, it was virtually impossible for one of over a dozen trawlers in the vicinity, or one of the coast stations tuned in on the distress frequencies, not to have heard it. This leads to the conclusion that whatever happened to GAUL was so sudden she had no time to broadcast a distress call. This conclusion is further strengthened by the fact that at the time she was presumed lost - between last being seen and failing to report on the 1630 hours schedule - her radio officer would have been on watch, and probably in the wireless room except for the period 1200 - 1230 hours when he would probably been at lunch.

Apart from one lifebuoy, no wreckage of any description or oil was found. This suggests strongly that GAUL was lost with her hull intact, and did not sink as a result of a collision, an explosion, or because her water-tight integrity was breached in any other violent way. The evidence is only consistent with the view that GAUL capsized and foundered. From this evidence, the finding of the Court was that the GAUL capsized and foundered as a result of taking a succession of heavy seas on her trawl deck when she was almost broadside to the sea, which initially caused her to heel over, and she had no time to recover before a subsequent wave or waves overcame her ability to right herself. She was probably coming round under helm from going down wind to coming head to wind at the time, and it seems likely that initially she was thrown so far over that those aboard were unable to transmit a distress message.

At the time the GAUL was lost I had a particular interest in following the evidence brought out at the Inquiry. Between 1969 and 1973 I had commanded similar types of ship to the GAUL (the MAMLA and KAMBA owned by State Fishing Corporation), and just prior to GAUL and her sisters being bought by B.U.T. I was approached by Captain Charles Hurst, at that time Marine Superintendent of Ranger Fishing Company, and offered the job of going out to St. Johns, Newfoundland, and joining RANGER CALLIOPE, one of GAUL's sisters, as mate to complete that trip, and later taking command of her on her next voyage. To me, and I suspect to many other experienced skippers, the Court findings did not ring true. There was no doubt that the weather was the cause of the loss, but if she was broadside to wind and sea, it was certainly not because she was in the process of coming round. I could not accept that a Skipper with Peter Nellist's ability and experience couldn't bring his ship round safely in heavy weather. It was suggested that because of frequent snow squalls, with visibility down to nil, he wouldn't see the huge approaching seas. This doesn't ring true either. In fact, it stinks. He was a careful, cautious skipper, and he wasn't going anywhere in particular. In the existing weather conditions he would have done what any other competent skipper would have done. He would have kept going down wind until the snow fall ceased, allowing him to see what seas were coming before starting to turn. Later, I will report evidence that was not available at the initial inquiry which suggests, in fact proves, that the GAUL could not have foundered unless her water-tight integrity had been breached.

With the conclusion of the Court of Inquiry, and publication of its findings, GAUL and her crew should have been laid to rest, and the media should have concentrated on more newsworthy items, but that didn't happen.

Dr. Lionel Rosen, who represented the relatives at the Inquiry.

Mr. (now Sir) Barry Sheen, Q.C., the Commissioner of Wrecks who headed the Inquiry.

41

CHAPTER 7

THE AFTERMATH

The inquiry into the loss of the GAUL took place from the 17th September 1974 and lasted until 11th October 1974, and its findings were published on 21st November 1974. Evidence were taken from 48 witnesses, and affidavits containing evidence from a dozen more witnesses were read to the Court. The Court found that "the Gaul capsized and foundered due to taking a succession of very heavy seas on her trawl deck when she was broadside to the sea, which initially caused her to heel over, and she had not time to recover before a subsequent wave or waves overcame her ability to right herself. It seems likely that she was thrown so far over that those aboard were unable to transmit a distress message".

The fishing community in Hull were still in shock over the disaster and refused to accept the findings of the Court. Rumours about a government cover up were widespread. A generally held belief was that GAUL was being used as a spy ship and had been arrested by the Russians and was being held in a Russian port. Dependants clung to this theory - it gave them hope that their men were still alive. But how plausible was it? Were British trawlers used as spy ships? Whether trawlers made specific voyages to sensitive areas for the specific purpose of spying seems unlikely, and had they done so, no doubt the lips of the personnel involved would have been sealed by the Official Secrets Act. What I can say is that trawlermen were approached by the Admiralty, and they did provide intelligence information. Some skippers were given cameras and asked to point them at Russian ships. Wireless operators were requested to listen and report on Russian radio communications. In the early 'fifties I was Mate of the trawler NORTHERN PRIDE working off the Murmansk Coast while the Russian fleet were exercising. On arrival back in Grimsby the Skipper and I were ordered to report to the Board of Trade Office where we were introduced to a naval intelligence officer who showed us a pack of silhouettes of various naval craft and asked us to identify the types of vessel we had seen. I have no reason to believe that this was an isolated case. It was a game both sides played during the Cold War. So far as the GAUL is concerned, on that fatal trip she was never within a hundred miles of the Russian coast and the weather conditions in the area she was in would have made it virtually impossible for a boarding party to have boarded her, and even if such an attempt had been made, she would have had ample time to use her radio. This seems to rule out any possibility that she was taken into a Russian port. Another theory put forward was that a submarine had surfaced underneath the GAUL, breaching her shell plating and causing her to sink. The chance of this happening is infinitesimal, and even if this had occurred there would have been traces. The GAUL had a double bottom extending for most of her length, and this double bottom consisted of fuel oil tanks. Had her bottom been ruptured oil would have escaped, and the slick would certainly have been sighted by the searching aircraft. The national press went to town and had a ball. One newspaper claimed that the GAUL'S wireless operator had been seen in a bar in Capetown, and Thames Television proposed to do a documentary "Spy Ship" based on the loss of the GAUL. British United Trawlers didn't like it and the Managing Director issued the following Internal Memorandum:

From: Graham Hellyer Date 14th October 1975
To: All B.U.T. Directors.
"Thames Television is screening a documentary on the investigation of the circumstances surrounding the disappearance of the British freezer trawler GAUL in two parts in the *This Week* slot, starting at 8.00 p.m. on Thursday, 16th October, and continuing the following week at 8.00 p.m. on Thursday, 23rd October.
The grapevine gossip is that Thames Television investigators are going to suggest that a nuclear submarine (Russian ?) surfaced under the GAUL and sank her and that the lifebuoy which was subsequently found off the Norwegian coast was planted there.
In spite of B.U.T. having very little enthusiasm for Thames Television's activities in this context, they have not been obstructive of this production, nor have they been excessively co-operative."
The day after the screening of the Thames Television programme the following telex was sent from Hull to the Chairman of Associated Fisheries, the parent company :

Assocfish LDN
Hellyer Hull 52162
Message for Mr.P.M.Tapscott, please. From Graham Hellyer.
Should it be necessary to issue a statement suggest the following :-
" The Department of Trade carried out a thorough Investigation into the disappearance of the GAUL and the Court of Inquiry which was subsequently held and lasted 15 days gave every opportunity for all possible causes for the vessel's loss to be thoroughly explored.
If the Department of Trade considers that further worthwhile evidence has come to light since their original investigations they will presumably take the appropriate action. In the meantime B.U.T. is not going to be a party to a continuing unofficial investigation by a section of the media, as in our opinion this will cause additional distress to the Dependants of the GAUL's 36-man crew, all of whom, with one exception, have accepted the Inquiry's findings that the vessel was lost with all hands."

Message ends. G.H. Hellyer Hull 52162 24.10.75 1205 BST

The above defines the attitude of the Owners of the Gaul. They wanted sleeping dogs to lie. Indeed, they preferred it. The value of the vessel and the legal costs of the Inquiry were covered by insurance, and the findings left the Company image untarnished. But this particular dog wouldn't go to sleep. Shortly after the findings of the Court of Inquiry were published an appeal in the Hull Daily Mail came from Mr. Leo Sheriden, a self-styled marine and aviation disaster investigator, for volunteers and sponsors to mount a land search along the coast of Jan Mayen Island for possible wreckage of the GAUL. He claimed later that 70 people, including nearly 40 trawlermen, had volunteered their services, and that two retired businessmen had offered financial backing but this would not be enough to cover the cost of the operation, and he (Sheriden) gauged that another £10,000 was needed to cover transport costs. The search party was scheduled to leave Hull on 1st May, 1974.

B.U.T were asked to contribute to the cost of the expedition but declined, and on 10th April 1974 a long letter was sent to Dependants setting out the reasons. At the end of the letter these reasons were summarised as follows:

(a) I consider the chances of finding any wreckage from GAUL are small.

(b) If any wreckage was found then the chances of this wreckage providing a worthwhile clue as to where or why the GAUL disappeared are very small indeed.

(c) I am not prepared to support any exercise that might keep the hopes of any dependant of the GAUL alive unless I thought there were some grounds to justify these hopes.

In the event, this expedition never got of the ground and Mr. Sheriden was arrested by the police and charged with obtaining £2,500 by deception from one of the sponsors of the expedition. He denied the charge and at the trial some months later was found not guilty. I believe that B.U.T.'s reasons for refusing to contribute to Mr. Sheriden's foolhardy, if well meaning, scheme were none other than given in the above letter, despite letters of criticism sent by Dependants to the company. My belief is based on a telex sent by Graham Hellyer to the Officer in Charge, Rescue Co - ordinating Centre, Bodoe at 1325 GMT on the 26th February, 1974, four days after the official search had been called off :

"We are very desirous of finding some wreckage from the GAUL in the hope that it might give us a clue to her fate. Do you consider it practical and worthwhile for us to charter a Norwegian helicopter or aircraft to carry out a further search for wreckage in the Northern Norwegian Fiords? Your advice on the effectiveness of a further search would be much appreciated."

Graham Hellyer B.U.T. Hull. Message ends. Bodeo R.C.C. replied at 2036 26th February 1974 thus :

"Your Telex at 1325 GMT this date refers. RCC Bodoe is also desirous of finding some wreckage that might give clue to the fate of the GAUL. As you know normal search and rescue missions have been called off. However, on the basis of your enquiry and what is mentioned above, this RCC will carry out a search with helicopters in all fiords and along all beaches from Svaerholt (N7100 E2630) and eastwards towards Vardo, starting tomorrow at first light. Report will be given on completion of SAR missions. Weather conditions must be suitable for this kind of search so missions may have to be postponed. RCC

Bodoe."

Hence B.U.T. had done all that could have been expected of them as regards the search, but Mr. Hellyer and B.U.T had more aggravation coming to them. The GAUL wouldn't go to sleep.

CHAPTER 8

THE LEGAL BATTLE

Early in 1979 there was an attempt in Hull to raise the money to mount an underwater search for the wreck of the GAUL and Mrs Shiela Doone, widow of Gaul's wireless operator, and other dependants, wrote to Hellyer Bros. on the 13th May 1979 asking the Company to make a donation towards this fund. On 18th May Mr. G.A. Hartley, a trawler manager employed by Hellyer, replied as follows:

"Dear Mrs Doone,
We are in receipt of your letter of the 13th May 1979 asking if we propose to contribute to the fund organised to search for our missing vessel GAUL.
As you know, it is assumed GAUL lies in very deep water in the Barents Sea, where the Royal Navy with all their experience of locating underwater objects have declined to search because of the extremely remote chance of finding the vessel.
Under these circumstances we do not think any useful purpose would be served by such a fund and would respectfully decline to contribute."
Yours sincerely for Hellyer Bros.Ltd. and signed G.A.Hartley

The author feels compelled to make comment on Mr. Hartley's letter. The term "very deep water" is relative. The probable depth of water the GAUL lies in is less than 200 fathoms, and probably nearer 150 fathoms. In oceanographic terms this is not "very deep water", and a modern survey vessel would experience no difficulty mounting a search in this depth of water. When he refers to the R.N declining to make a search, what he should have said, maybe, is that the R.N had disbanded, or greatly reduced, its capability to conduct survey operations. Its policy at that time was to contract such work to private survey companies. When a jet fighter came down in the North Sea a private survey company's vessel and personnel were chartered to find and recover the wreckage, and when the Admiralty proposed to rechart the Western Approaches to establish the best deep water channel for the big oil tankers expected to use the oil terminal at Sullom Voe, again the work was entrusted to private companies. In fact, I was employed for over two years as Chief Navigating Officer on survey vessels contracted to conduct this operation. Now consider 'the extremely remote chance of finding the vessel.' Over the years a great many U.K. and Norwegian trawlers have pulled North Cape Bank about. There are Skippers who know this bank like you know your own back garden, and have charted every rock, hole and obstruction in the area. When their gear comes fast on an obstruction they hadn't found before, naturally they ask themselves what it is, and note its position for future reference. A number of Skippers claim to have come fast on the GAUL, one claimed that blue paint marks were embedded in his trawl door (the GAUL's hull was painted blue), and a Norwegian Skipper believes he found the wreck of the GAUL and has a recording of it on sonar recording paper. In a another letter to Mrs Doone commenting on the later case, Mr. Hartley wrote ".... other people think the recording showed fish, not a vessel. We are unable to verify the skipper's assessment." The truth of the matter is that finding the GAUL would not have presented too many problems. Collecting the positions of the trawler skippers' reported findings would have limited the search area and once found on sonar it would have been a simple matter to get a camera down to verify the wreck. Look at what was done in the case of the TITANIC where the wreck was in really deep water, and how the wreck of the DERBYSHIRE was found, again in much deeper water than the GAUL is presumed to lie in. I sincerely believe I could have found the GAUL in a month. All that was required was the will and the financial backing. But as I propose to show, the last thing the GAUL's owners wanted at this time was the wreck on camera for fear of what the pictures would show.

In 1978, or sooner, a group of the dependants consulted Graham and Rosen, a firm of Hull solicitors who were specialists in marine law, with a view to suing the owners of the GAUL for compensation on the grounds of negligence. An application for legal aid was made and granted. Subsequently a writ was served to Hellyer Bros. and naming the GAUL's builders, Brooke Marine Ltd., as second defendants, who passed it on to U.K. Trawlers Mutual Insurance Company Ltd., the vessel's underwriters. Solicitors for the Insurance Company, A.M.Jackson & Co., engaged Michael Thomas QC and David Steel to advise on the defence to the negligence charge. In order to prove negligence the plaintiffs would presumably have to cast doubts on the findings of the Court of Inquiry into the loss, and this led to intensive investigation into the GAUL's stability. Rosen engaged Dr. Corlett of Burnet Corlett Partners Ltd., a firm of marine consultants to look at the GAUL's design and stability. Dr. Corlett's initial line of attack was to attempt to show that the arrangement of scuppers on the GAUL's trawl deck was inadequate or wrongly positioned to allow water from this deck to escape, that in bad weather it could be expected that a large amount of water would be continuously on this deck, and that the effective area of these scuppers did not comply with regulations in force at the time.

B.U.T engaged the services of Alan William Gilfillan, head of the naval architecture section of Y-ARD, a Glasgow firm of marine consultants, and John Andreas Tvedt, a naval architect. Brooke Marine called on the services of Laurence Draper, a weather and wave expert on the staff of the Institute of Oceanographic Sciences, and George Donaldson, their own chief naval architect. Between them they had little difficulty in refuting Dr. Corlett's assumptions, and Michael Thomas was of the opinion that the defence had a good case. However, while this battle was going on, the Department of Trade and Industry instructed the National Marine Institute to investigate fully the seaway stability of Gaul. N.M.I. carried out extensive tank tests and model experiments in the Solent simulating various sea conditions, some worse than were likely to have been encountered by the GAUL, and sea tests on the ARAB, one of the GAUL's sisters. The result of these tests showed conclusively that the GAUL could not possibly have been lost by the presence of water, however much, on her decks. Their calculations also showed that with her watertight integrity intact GAUL would still have a righting lever with a heel of 90 degrees. In other words, GAUL could not have foundered due to shipping water alone. She must have had a large quantity of water inside her hull. The marine experts employed by the GAUL's owners were unable to cast doubt on the main points of the N.M.I. (Project No.207001 Investigation into the Seaway Stability of MT GAUL) Report and were forced to accept them. This development threw a completely new light on the case and was a cause of concern for the defendants. It was now a different ball game. Dr. Corlett apparently abandoned his original line of attack and started work on a new report. The plaintiff advised that they were no longer pressing on with any case against Brooke Marine, the shipbuilders, and the said builders were excluded from the proceedings.

On the 29th September 1978 a conference was held with Michael Thomas Q.C. and David Steel Junior Counsel. Those present were Admiral Branson, M.D. of U.K. Trawler Insurance Company, Admiral Ievers, also of the insurance company, G. Hellyer, A.W. Gilfillan and J.A.Tvedt, marine experts, and the solicitors representing the insurance company. The following are extracts from notes of this conference taken by G.F.Lambert (Ref.GFL/AB) a solicitor with A.M.Jackson & Co. Discussion centred on what could be done to attack the N.M.I. Report, and it was thought that the opinion of an expert on tank testing was needed. Someone who could read the report and say whether the tests had been thoroughly carried out and also comment on any tests that had been omitted. The naval architects suggested various names and it was decided that one from Copenhagen should be contacted by Mr. Gilfillan, and failing him, one at Gothenburg should be contacted by Mr. Tvedt. (Note. In the event Professor Falkemo, a recognised international expert in Naval Architecture and Tank Testing from Gothenburg got the job and in his report he confirmed the view of N.M.I. that the GAUL was a seaworthy vessel and could not have sunk unless her watertight integrity had been breached.)

Michael Thomas Q.C. expressed the opinion that on the basis of N.M.I. Report a Court could, and might well come to the conclusion that this was the only possible cause that had been demonstrated, because everybody else said the ship could not be sunk by any other means, therefore flooding and water inside the vessel was the only possible cause, and this would lead to a finding of negligence on the owners. There were grounds to argue against this but he feared that there could be an adverse decision. The question of a possible settlement was discussed and it was pointed out that in July 1977 the advice was that there was a good case but this was before the N.M.I. Report. The question of any settlement would depend on whether the N.M.I. Report could be efficiently attacked. For the above reasons Graham and Rosen should be asked politely for their views on quantum of claims at this stage so as to be in a position to have up-to-date figures ready for a further meeting perhaps in November.

The following text is taken from a report sent to Admiral Branson by A.M.

Jackson & Co. (Ref GLF/BAB) and dated 12th January 1979.
Trial Date. This has been fixed for the 2nd of October next in the Admiralty Court in London,

"Probably before Donaldson J., and three weeks have been allowed.
Mr. L. Draper. Brooke Marine have produced a report from Draper, an internationally recognised weather expert. This enlarges on the evidence he gave at the original Inquiry into the loss of GAUL, and confirms his opinion that although the weather was bad, it was not so bad that a vessel like GAUL should have been overwhelmed.
Professor Falkemo. Has delivered a report and has answered questions set by our Junior Counsel, David Steel. He has various minor criticisms of the N.M.I. Report but confirms that GAUL could not have sunk unless her water-tight integrity was breached. He considers that there is a distinct possibility, as our other experts do, that GAUL was overwhelmed from ahead i.e. by water entering the bridge superstructure.
Experts' Opinions. The theory we will put forward is that it is more likely that GAUL was lost because of damage to the bridge by a heavy wave, possibly injuring those on the bridge, flooding it, and cutting out all electrics, including radio. However, following that there has to be entry of water in considerable quantities for her to lose stability and sink. Gilfillan and Tvedt are looking into this.
Conference with Counsel. Michael Thomas Q.C. indicated he thought it was a good case to run but pointed out the reluctance of a Court to deprive Widows of a claim and there could be a leaning to find for the Plaintiff. He thought in all strictness the Court ought to find there was no liability on the Owners, but it was not an easy case to run and would be expensive. He felt that it was sensible advice that enquiries should be made to see if a negotiated settlement could be possible. A settlement at not more than half the limit of liability might well be attractive to Owners and their Insurers. (A settlement at this level would be about £75,000 plus about £40,000 costs).
Financial Implications. An assessment of the value of the total claims, including interest made by me (G.F.Lambert) is approximately £270,000 but the limitation fund of the Gaul, with the addition of interest from the date of the casualty, is about £150,000.
If it was accepted by the Court that there was water on the factory deck combined with the door leading to this deck open, that would be negligence of the crew, not the Owners. (Author's note. It can be argued that an employer is responsible for an employee's negligence, but to cancel the owner's right to limit liability it would have to be shown that they were directly and deliberately negligent).
The costs are going to be high because there are a lot of experts being employed. To date each party will have incurred not less than £10,000 worth of costs and expenses, and if the case proceeds to trial and lasts 15 days there will be a further minimum of £40,000 total costs. If the case is fought and the Owners are held liable but still entitled to limit liability there will be something like

£220,000 to pay. If the Owners were not entitled to limit their liability this would rise to £340,000. These figures are divisible between your Company and the Re-Insurers, details of which will be known to you. Settlement Possibilities. I (G.F.Lambert) have had a short discussion with the Plaintiff's Solicitor (Rosen) and can tell you that he is fully aware of the difficulty of establishing liability and he undoubtedly will be willing to recommend a settlement at something under the limit of liability of £150,000. Of course, I did not make any concrete offer, but my feelings are that a settlement might be arranged on a 50% basis, i.e. £75,000 plus costs. Doubtless the Plaintiff's Solicitor will want to take his Counsel's advice, and he may want to wait until Dr. Corlett has reported again. He also indicated he might have difficulty in convincing some of his Clients. If any offer is made it must be on the basis that it must be accepted by all Graham & Rosen's claimants. I have little doubt that the other three cases represented by other firms of solicitors would follow suit because they just do not have the knowledge to run the case themselves.

My own view is that we ought to win this case but I agree with Michael Thomas that a settlement of not more than 50% of the limitation fund is an attractive one. One of the advantages of making an offer is that the Plaintiff, being legally aided, the offer must be reported to the Law Society Legal Aid Fund. They are aware of the cost of running the case because they will have had to authorise considerable payments of experts' fees, et cetera. The possibility of getting the costs recovered and damages may result in some pressure being put to encourage a settlement. If an opening offer is to be made I suggest a basis of not more than one-third because they would undoubtedly want to push me up. I think negotiations would take some time and should be opened as soon as possible if those are to be my instructions."

Although I do not have the details it would seem that an offer was made. Bear in mind that in the Hull fishing community a lot of bitterness existed over the GAUL tragedy. 36 of their men had been lost and no satisfactory explanation had been forthcoming. The dependants wanted blood, B.U.T.'s blood, and they relished the prospect of a showdown in the Admiralty Court. No doubt Dr. Lionel Rosen did his utmost to persuade his clients to allow him to negotiate the best possible deal, but his advice went unheeded, and the offer was rejected.

Presumably, on hearing that an offer of settlement had been made, the Law Society cut off legal aid, and the Plaintiffs lacked the funds to continue the case, and it never reached the floor of the Courtroom. B.U.T. was off the hook and Rosen was left with the unenviable task of negotiating the best deal he could get with no weapons in his armoury.

To conclude, the following is a transcript of a note from Mr. L.H.Swaine, Financial Director to Mr. Graham Hellyer dated 18th February 1980:

1. In 1977, having regard to estimated costs, the Mutual made an approach to Rosen asking what figure Rosen had in mind as compensation. The Mutual had in mind that, with limitation, the figure could be about £120,000, and without limitation could be as high as £500,000.

Rosen's reply indicated £180,000 based on claims then notified.

2. In June 1979 Graham & Rosen made an approach to UKMIC's solicitors for a settlement, having realised that the dependants were now unlikely to win their case and suggested the settlement be based on the minimum allowed by the Law Reform Act. Based on claims then notified this gave £15,000 to the dependants. An offer of £30,000 was made to include Graham & Rosen costs. Graham & Rosen indicated that their costs were substantially higher than £15,000 and the matter was finally settled including late claims as to £16,730.94 to the dependants and £24,250 costs.

3. There were 19 claims by dependants.

There seems little doubt that had Lionel Rosen been allowed to use his skill and negotiate while the threat of a Courtroom battle existed, together with the resultant large costs involved, and the content of the N.M.I. Report was still relevant, he could have struck a much better deal for his clients. Some aspects of the route to a settlement remain unclear. Sarah Boseley, of the *Guardian,* put a lot of effort into trying to unravel the mystery. The content of the M.N.I. Report which destroyed the findings of the official inquiry was never made public. Why? Shiela Doone, widow of GAUL's wireless operator, and Beryl Betts, sister of one of the lost men, told Sarah they had no knowledge of it. Dr Rosen has been dead for some years, and the firm have no records of the case. Geoffrey Lambert, now retired, was the legal eagle with Andrew M.Jackson, the underwriter's solicitors, who handled the case. He told Sarah "I don't suppose they (the dependants) would be told about it. They didn't know about it, I'm sure." Graham Hellyer had earlier tried to get an out of court settlement. In a personal letter to Paul Tapscott, Chairman of B.U.T., dated January 1980 he regretted that most of the money had gone to lawyers. "In my opinion the dependants have finished up with far less than they would have got had they settled out of court three years ago, but in no way is that the fault of B.U.T."

CHAPTER 9

HOW DID THE GAUL SINK

We now have all the evidence we are likely ever to get about the loss of the Gaul, at least until a thorough survey is done of the wreck. Let us summarise the facts.

1. The weather was very bad at the time but not, according to the experts, so bad that GAUL should have been overwhelmed.
2. Whatever happened, it was so quick that GAUL was unable to use her radio, or her radio was put out of action.
3. The N.M.I. Report disproved the findings of the Court of Inquiry. Water on her deck could not have reduced her stability to the point where she would have been unable to recover.
4. If we accept the validity of the N.M.I. Report, and leading experts who were called in to attack it had to accept it, then water in large quantities must have entered the GAUL's hull.
5. Absence of any wreckage or any oil slick seem to rule out the possibility of the hull being ruptured by violent means e.g. mine or collision. The implication of this is that the hull was intact, and water entered the vessel from somewhere above the waterline.

If the cause of water entering the ship was due to wind and sea, for example, the wheelhouse being stove in, or damage to the deck or a hatch, there would be no negligence, but if water had entered through a door or other opening that had been left open there would.

Naturally, the owners of the GAUL wanted to show that the former was the case and the efforts of Gilfillan and Tvedt were directed to this end.

The theory they advanced was that while the ship was head to wind a big sea had come aboard, and flooded the bridge, shorting all the electrics including the radio, and maybe injuring the personnel on the bridge. Then, while the ship was being brought round to sail before the wind while repairs were carried out, she was swamped by heavy seas coming aboard. There is one snag to this argument. It does not explain how the large amount of water required to nullify the vessel's stability entered the vessel's hull. Perhaps, had the case gone to Court, they could have come up with the answer. In the Y-ARD CONFIDENTIAL REPORT 2424/78 Y 1603 dated April 1978 and signed by Gilfillan and Tvedt three cases where a ship had the wheelhouse damaged in heavy weather were referred to.

1. Motor Trawler VADSOGUTT: On 23rd November 1974 M.T. VADSOGUTT was dodging on North Cape Bank in a NW gale force 8-9 with heavy seas.

Extract from her log:

1645. Took on board heavy sea which broke three window panes and a lot of sea came into the wheelhouse and major portions of the instruments were destroyed. Obtained contact with M.T. HELGOFJORD when on its way towards land. He was prepared to wait until we got the wheelhouse windows blocked up and he accompanied us towards land. Seaman Nils Pedersen got a cut on the head.

Damage Report: Bridge Front.
1. off sliding window shattered and the frame broken.
2. off fixed windows with electrical heating shattered, one frame broken, the other bent.
3. clear-view windows shattered and frames broken. A screen plate built over the windows on the outside of the bridge front, and railings were bent. There was extensive damage to electrics, including radios, but the V.H.F. radio was still functioning. Some water had leaked through the wheelhouse floor into the accommodation below and damage was caused to floor coverings.

2. SEA BRUIN: From Norwegian Journal of Commerce and Shipping, 21.5.77.: On Viking Bank in a hurricane (the drilling rig Deep Sea Saga measured the wind force at 90 knots) the supply boat SEA BRUIN shipped a heavy sea which smashed four windows in the front of the wheelhouse and two in the back. The bridge was filled with sea and water ran down through the deckhouse into the cabins on the deck below. Radar, Decca radio transmitter, R.D.F. and other electronic equipment were put completely out of action. Contact with another supply boat, KING SUPPLIER, was made with a V.H.F. hand set and she accompanied SEA BRUIN into Alesund.

3. DANA REGINA: a large ferry, suffered wheelhouse damage leading to minor fires.

The Y-ARD Report sums up by suggesting that in the event of the GAUL's wheelhouse being swamped the following sequence of events could have occurred:
1. All radio equipment, auto alarm and command systems put out of action.
2. Temporary loss of main engine due to short circuiting of emergency stop button, leading to loss of main engine power and blackout at shaft driven alternator.
3. Temporary loss of steering.
4. Even if no personal injury occurred it would take some time to restore control and power. Most likely she would have to turn stern to the weather whilst temporary repairs were made.
5. In the course of this manoeuvre it is possible for large quantities of water to have reached the trawl deck leading to the loss of the vessel.   This is a good try but an expert can pick holes in it, and we will try to do just that. Then we will suggest possible causes of the loss which cater for ALL the known facts.

First of all, the above summary does not account for one important point. Water had to enter the GAUL in large quantities for her stability to be reduced to a catastrophic level - about 170 tons (N.M.I. Report) - and it is doubtful if that amount of water could have run into the ship through the wheelhouse. It didn't happen in any of the cases the report referred to, and had it happened on any previous occasion Gilfillan and Tvelt would certainly have referred to it.

Secondly, suppose the above sequence of events 1 - 3 had occurred. The vessel would have been unable to turn stern to weather until power had been restored to engines and steering. What would have happened is that the ship would have settled broad side to the wind, or nearly so. Which tack she laid on would depend on where the wind was relative to her bow when control was lost.

There is one possibility the Y-ARD Report ignores, probably because they (and B.U.T) prefer it not to be considered. When a trawler is sailing down wind the accommodation becomes uncomfortably hot. It is a common occurrence for a crew member to fix open the door into the accommodation companion way to cool the place down. Don't take my word for it. Ask any trawler skipper.

In the GAUL the door leading into the forecastle was on the port side just fore side of the trawl winch. There was also a door leading to the factory deck sited in the after end of the engine casing on the starboard side. Note that no mention of this door was made at the Official Inquiry. Both these doors are not visible from the bridge. My contention is that one of these doors was open. If you accept that, (and at the time of writing there is no proof one way or the other) we can easily explain the loss of the GAUL.

The N.M.I. Report draws attention to other openings on the starboard side which could admit water if the vessel developed a list. There were two offal chutes on the factory deck closed by counter-balancing weights that would allow water to enter the vessel with a twenty degree list, and there was a ventilator on the inboard side of the starboard funnel which would allow water to enter the vessel with a list of between 30 and 40 degrees. The N.M.I. Report stresses that water coming on to the trawl deck would be trapped in the vicinity of the door in the engine casing, and that with water on the factory deck the vessel would list to starboard.

1. Suppose that Y-ARD's supposition that the bridge had been flooded and control had been lost. The ship would come off the wind and lay broadside to. Professor Falkemo had calculated that the period of GAUL's roll was 11-12 seconds. Mr. Draper calculated the significant period of the wind waves between 10.30 and 16.30 (the period GAUL was presumed to have been lost) to be about the same. This means that GAUL would be in resonance with the waves, and as a consequence would roll heavily, the angle of roll increasing with each roll. She would probably ship heavy water on the trawl deck, and a large volume of water would flood through the open door down to the factory deck. As the vessel listed there would be a further ingress of water through the waste chutes and the ventilator. The weight and free surface effect of this large quantity of water would cancel GAUL's ability to right itself and she would capsize. It would happen very quickly and there would be no time to use the radio.

2. Now suppose that GAUL wasn't head to wind - she was sailing down wind. The same argument applies. If she took a big sea up the ramp, or over the quarter, again water would flood through the open door and down to the factory deck. The steering compartment is on the centre line of the after end of this deck. The weight of water would increase the vessel's trim by the stern and the water would have flooded into the steering compartment and shorted the electrics or broken the hydraulic pipes thus causing loss of steering. The same sequence of events outlined above would occur.

I suggest that my theory is more in keeping with the facts known to us, and personally I believe that when a diver or a camera examines the GAUL thoroughly, that door will be found to be open. And if so, negligence would be proved. I don't know what the legal position would be. The dependants accepted a settlement and the owning company no longer exists.

The trawl deck (starboard) showing door to factory deck (the "Arab"). Photo courtesy Royal Institute of Naval Architects.

The trawl deck (starboard) showing funnel with ventilators (the "Arab"). Photo courtesy Royal Institute of Naval Architects.

CHAPTER 10

THE NATIONAL MARITIME INSTITUTE REPORT

This Report - INVESTIGATION INTO THE STABILITY OF MFV GAUL IN A SEAWAY (Project 207001) - was compiled by the National Maritime Institute (formerly Ship Division, NPL) at the request of the Department of Trade in a letter from the Surveyor General dated 13 March 1975, and was funded by the Ship Operations Sub-Committee SMTRB (Ref: MS 92/12/08 and MS 92/12/09).

An extensive range of tests and experiments was carried out using a model of the GAUL comprising the following:

1. Rough Water Tests at the model tank of the National Maritime Institute.
2. Wind Tunnel experiments.
3. Rough Water Tests in the Solent in conjuction with British Hovercraft.
4. Manoeuvring Tests in the Haslar Model Tank.
5. Full scale tests at sea on the M.T. ARAB, one of GAUL's sisterships.

It was expected that these further investigations would lead to improved trawler safety and reduce the risk of a similar tragedy ever occurring again. Sea tests were conducted on the ARAB, one of GAUL's sister ships, and flooding experiments were carried out on a model of the GAUL in the Solent. The work resulted in a massive document which included six interim reports and a final report. The following text is derived from Interim Report 6 which also summarises the five previous interim reports, and was delivered to the Department of Trade on 15 June 1977. To avoid any possible distortion of the Report's conclusions I give large parts verbatim.

The initial model experiments were carried out in the Solent with a quantity of water corresponding to 60 tonnes on the factory deck. This failed to endanger the vessel, in spite of its reduced righting stability. This was considered to be due to the intact state of the model preventing any entry of water into the factory deck, engine room, deck houses or bridge. However, it was clear that water coming on to the trawl deck tended to accumulate on the starboard side just aft of the funnel where, on the GAUL, there is an access door to the factory deck. As a result of this observation it was decided to inspect the ARAB to obtain a better understanding of the sequence of any flooding that could have taken place below the trawl deck prior to the loss of the GAUL. After a general examination of the ship all the openings where flooding could have taken place to a greater or lesser extent were noted. These are listed as follows:

A. Openings on the Trawl Deck.
  1. The access to the factory deck from the trawl deck is through a watertight door in the funnel casing on the starboard side. This door faces aft and could not

be seen from the bridge.

2. Just forward of the factory deck access door and facing inboard is a louvred ventilator for the factory deck. This louvre can be closed by a metal door although the top half is usually left open at sea.

3. The engine room ventilators are on the inboard side of the starboard funnel and are much higher above the deck than the louvre mentioned above.

4. The engine room escape hatch is built in the starboard funnel casing next to the factory deck access. This door would normally be closed at sea.

5. There are two hydraulic fish loading hatches sited at the top of the stern ramp. When closed these hatches are unlikely to be a major source of flooding, although on the first sea trials on the ARAB water was seen coming through the closed hatches and down the fish chutes to the factory deck.

6. A deck hatch on the starboard side allows access to the net store, and steering gear and liver oil plant compartments. This hatch would be normally closed at sea.

7. At the forward end of the trawl deck and facing inboard are two louvred ventilators for the factory deck, one either side. These can be closed completely by metal doors.

8. Just aft of the forward ventilator on the starboard side is an access hatch to the fish meal hold which would normally be closed while at sea.

9. The access door to the engine room is at the after end of the funnel casing on the port side. This door would normally be closed at sea.

10. Just forward of the engine room door is a louvred ventilator for the factory deck which can be closed completely by a metal door.

B. Openings in the Ship's Side.

Two chutes for the discharge of duff and offal overboard were fitted on the starboard side of the factory space. These chutes were closed with a counterbalanced weight but water could enter the vessel through them when a heel of about 20 degrees to starboard took place.

C. Observations on the Factory Deck.

The factory deck has a 0.6 metre coaming at frame 45 separating the processing plant from the fish freezing machinery and fish hold.

Access to the engine room is through two doors in the engine room casing sited on the port side. The forward door is normally kept open and the after one closed. The sill height above the deck for both of these doors is 0.635 metres.

Access to the factory deck at the forward end is sited next to the loading hatch leading to the fish hold. Stop/Start buttons for the factory drainage pumps are situated immediately above this entrance. An alternative set of controls is situated in the engine room.

There is an entrance to the liver oil plant, net store and steering gear compartment at the after end of the factory deck. The sill height of this entrance is 0.635 metres and about 0.15 metres to the other doors. The centreline of the steering gear pumps was about 0.38 metres above deck.

The drain wells and the pumps, which were not submersible, were sited at the aft end of the factory deck.

A Sequence of Progressive Flooding.

On the assumption that progressive flooding of the factory deck could have taken place the most likely sequence of events is described below. The main sources of flooding are internal and external to the factory deck.

1. Internal Sources: In the event of forgetting to turn off the processing pumps, or by a pump running in an uncontrolled manner, 110 - 150 tonnes of water could have accumulated on the factory deck if these pumps were running unattended for about two hours. In this case water would flow in through wash deck and processing machinery lines.

2. External Sources: In the event of the access door and adjacent ventilator on the starboard side of the trawl deck being left open an additional 30 tonnes of water a minute could have entered the factory deck every time a substantial quantity of water reached the access doorway. This inflow of water was calculated by Weir formula assuming a mean depth of water of 0.6 metres above the access door sill. On this assumption it would take about six periods of one minute duration to accumulate 180 tons of water on the factory deck.

In the above hypothesis water would accumulate on the factory deck either from internal or external sources or a combination of both. Assuming that a certain amount of water was already on the factory deck and that the vessel developed a list to starboard, then water would enter the open access doorway on the starboard side every time substantial quantities of water reached this area (i.e. every time she shipped a sea). The model experiments on the Solent had shown that with water on the factory deck the vessel tended to list to starboard and that in this condition green water was more likely to reach the trawl deck from over the after bulwark. If this initial list was noticed by the officer on the bridge a change of course to correct heel might have been attempted. In these circumstances water would not enter the engine room from the door on the port side of the factory deck on account of its position and higher door sill. The water on the factory deck would accumulate at the after end and not reach the fish hold loading hatch on the centre line at frames 56 - 60. With a significant heel to starboard water would flow aft through the liver oil plant and into the net store and steering gear compartment where it would put the steering gear out of action. If the starboard heel was big enough water would enter the engine room vents and rubbish chutes. The resultant increase in floodwater would increase the trim by the stern and increase the vulnerability of openings in the starboard side already admitting flood water and capsize would be rapid thereafter.

In order to confirm the correctness of the above hypothesis the model was modified to allow flooding to take place from a number of selected openings. The following modifications were made to the model:

1. The access door and companion-way to the factory deck on the starboard side of the trawl deck. These openings would allow flooding of the factory deck to take place once water reached the trawl deck in substantial quantities.

2. A small opening just forward of the above access door to represent a partially closed louvred ventilator to the factory deck.

3. A hollow metal funnel fitted with ventilator grilles on the inboard face on the starboard side. This funnel would allow flooding to take place down to the trawl deck level at very large angles of heel. On the actual ship water would enter the engine room through the funnel ventilators but this could not be allowed on the model because of the apparatus and instrumentation.

4. The access door to the liver oil plant and net store on the starboard side of the factory deck. This opening would allow flooding of these compartments from water accumulating at the after end of the factory deck, and then flowing aft with increasing stern trim. Flooding of the steering gear compartment was not allowed on the model because the steering gear controls were sited here.

5. The simulated bridge windows at the front and side were replaced with openings to allow local flooding to take place on the assumption of wave damage to the windows. This would make the model less intact at big angles of heel.

The Flooding Experiments

The model was again taken to Totland Bay, Isle of Wight, for experiments in waves corresponding to severe sea conditions. These experiments were conducted in the Solent between Burst Castle and Yarmouth and were carried out in November 1976 and March 1977. The object was to investigate the behaviour of the GAUL model in a partially flooded condition with various openings on the trawl deck and in the starboard funnel. The main difference between these and previous experiments was in the larger quantity of water that was placed on the factory deck and in the provision of openings in the structure. These openings would allow further flooding to take place once water reached the trawl deck in substantial quantities and when the model took large angles of heel.

The experiments were concentrated on quartering and following sea conditions with 100 tonnes of water placed on the factory deck. In the initial experiments the bridge window openings were sealed to prevent any ingress of water while the model was being towed or when under way. Also, the access door to the factory deck was sealed until the experiments were in progress. The experiments were made in a condition corresponding to that of the loss of GAUL with a mean draft of 4.1 metres and a trim relative to the datum line of 0.61 metres. The trim in the flooding experiments was based on the value estimated by Y-ARD at the time of the formal investigation and with a metacentric height of 0.646 metres prior to water being placed on the factory deck. A portable wave buoy was deployed from the launch PROTECTOR at the beginning and end of the test run and wave spectra were obtained from the wave records.

At the start of the first test run during the November trials the propeller shaft became fouled with a nylon line and the test was aborted. However, at the time the model was positioned in a quartering sea and the waves were severe enough to allow water to break on the trawl deck and enter the factory deck. In the first instance this was assisted by the list to starboard caused by the water placed on the factory deck. In a short space of time the model listed further to starboard as more water entered the factory deck and eventually listed to an angle of about 70 degrees. On returning to shore the water in the factory deck was weighed and this corresponded to 180 tonnes of water on the ship. In other words about 80 tonnes of water had entered the factory deck through the access door on the trawl deck. The interval of time in which the model accumulated this extra water was calculated to be about 20 - 30 minutes for the ship. There was no doubt that the model was severely endangered in this condition and recovery from this position if this had occurred on the GAUL would have been most unlikely.

Similar experiments to those described above were carried out in March 1977 and similar tendencies of behaviour were observed. The sea conditions were less severe than those encountered previously and as a result less water entered the factory deck. On this occasion an amount corresponding to 40 tonnes entered the factory deck in an interval of about 30 - 40 minutes for the ship.

Both of the above flooding experiments demonstrated that with water already on the factory deck, causing the vessel to list to starboard, water in substantial quantities would reach the trawl deck and enter the access door to the factory deck. Furthermore when the total quantity of water on the factory deck approached 180 tonnes the vessel would list to over 70 degrees and be most severely endangered. As a result the vessel would undoubtedly capsize after admitting more flood water from the openings on the starboard size and as progressive flooding took place throughout the ship.

On the GAUL nearly all the openings, such as the access door to the factory deck, the ventilators and the rubbish chutes were all positioned on the starboard side. Moreover the access door was sited so that it could not be seen from the bridge. Due to the asymmetry of the deckhouses on the trawl deck less reserve buoyancy was available on the starboard side than the port side. This made it possible to effectively trap water under the starboard engine casing because of the absence of a deckhouse in this area and the access door could have been under a metre or more of water. The starboard funnel was used mainly as a ventilator making it possible for water to enter the engine room at large angles of heel. Water would flood aft into the steering compartment and put the steering gear out of action. With an angle of heel of about 50 degrees the main engine would probably cease to function thus cutting off all light and power. Of course it is not known how many of the above factors contributed to the loss of the GAUL because there were no surviving witnesses but the vessel would have been more seaworthy if the above features had been reconsidered in the early stages of design.

In so far as the experiments made in this investigation represent realistic conditions, IT WOULD APPEAR THAT THE LOSS OF STABILITY CAUSED BY WATER ON THE TRAWL DECK WOULD NOT BE SUFFICIENT ON ITS OWN TO CAUSE CAPSIZE. The most serious loss of stability, and one that would be sufficient to cause GAUL to capsize and founder, is that of considerable amounts of water present simultaneously on the trawl and factory decks. This condition might arise from the result of a combination of flooding from the processing pumps on the factory deck and from water flooding through the access door on the starboard side of the trawl deck.

It is perfectly clear that this report completely destroys the findings of the Official Inquiry into the casualty that " GAUL capsized and foundered due to taking a succession of heavy seas on her trawl deck ......". GAUL could not have capsized and foundered on account of water on her decks, no matter how much, unless her watertight integrity had been breached and a large quantity of water had entered her hull.

What is not so clear is why the Department of Trade, having commissioned the report, declined to make its findings public. The N.M.I. report which contained evidence that rendered the findings of its own Official Inquiry invalid has never been published. And publication may have made a great deal of difference to the lives of a lot of people. The dependants of the crewmen of the GAUL have spent the last 24 years in a state of Limbo in doubt as to the fate of their menfolk. Now it is far too late for reports to move them. They have been told too many lies and too many half truths to be swayed. Mistrust and suspicion is too deeply engraved to be removed. But if the report had been made available to them in 1977 when it was first delivered to the Department of Trade it just might have convinced them that the sea had taken their men. Suppression of the evidence contained in the report could also have made a profound difference to the dependants' finances. Recall that in their attempt to claim damages for negligence from the GAUL's owners, legal aid was withdrawn and they were unable to take their case to the Admiralty Court. It is probable that had they been in possession of this evidence the Law Society would have made legal aid available. The solicitor acting for them has passed away, but in an interview with Sarah Boseley of the *Guardian* newspaper, Geoffrey Lambert, the lawyer acting for GAUL's underwriters stated "They wouldn't have been told. I am sure they didn't know about it." Mrs Shiela Doone, widow of GAUL's wireless operator, and other dependants told Sarah that the only report on the ship's stability that they were told about was the one disclosed at the Inquiry in September 1974. Had the case gone to Court it is probable that the findings would have favoured the plaintiffs. In that case Geoffrey Lambert had calculated there would have been about £220,000 to pay if limitation was allowed, which would rise to £340,000 if not. One thing for sure. The Department of Trade should reopen the case of the loss of the GAUL to take into consideration the evidence that has been kept under wrap for so many years. The time is long overdue for a full expedition to be mounted to survey her wreck. The task would not be difficult. I sincerely believe I could have found her in a month. It can be safely assumed that she was lost between 1109 hours when she was in contact with Wick Radio and 1630 hours when she failed to report on schedule. We can establish her position at 1100 hours (she was in sight of the SWANELLA), we know she was dodging, and we know the wind direction. Giving her a maximum speed over the ground of 7 knots down wind and 3 knots head to, we can construct a box with her last known position as a focal point. The box would be 50 miles long and we could allow 15 miles either side of the line in the direction of the wind drawn through her last known position. The GAUL would have had to be in that box. 1,500 square miles of seabed would have required a lot of searching but this area could have been reduced considerably. We have the positions the liferaft covers were found in 1977 and 1979. We also have the positions that trawler skippers claim to have snagged the wreck with their gear. One Norwegian skipper even claims to have a recording of the wreck on sonar paper. The Decca readings of these positions will be available. In fact, skippers working on North Cape Bank have reported a wreck that was not there before the storm which took the GAUL, and they have charted its position. They are sure it is the GAUL and have recorded the Decca readings. These readings are RED C 16.1 GREEN F 34.5. The geographical co-ordinates of the Decca position are 72 degrees 5 minutes North, 25 degrees 6 minutes East.

Some of the Hull once trawler owning companies are now involved in marine survey work. They have the ships and the equipment to do the job. I, and I am sure a number of Hull ex-trawler skippers would volunteer their services to crew a ship. It may be that the free publicity generated by media attention would amply repay the cost to the company that set out to find the GAUL. One thing is sure, it is the only way that those widows and children will ever know peace of mind.

Since the foregoing pages were written, Anglia Television Ltd., in conjunction with NRK, the Norwegian TV Company, chartered a survey vessel to look for the GAUL. Using the positions given by trawler skippers who had claimed to have come fast on the wreck, or had seen it on sonar, a search was made using side-scan sonar. Within six hours of the sonar fish being launched the wreck was found An underwater camera was sent down, and the pictures sent back to the mother vessel established without doubt that the wreck was indeed the GAUL. The programme was televised on Channel 4 in November 1997. It confirmed what trawler skippers had known for years - where the wreck was. Much of the programme focused on the 'Cold War" angle, but on dealing with how the GAUL came to founder the camera provided vital evidence. It showed that the bridge front was not damaged and that the bridge windows were intact, thus destroying the owner's marine experts' hypothesis that water could have entered the hull through a damaged bridge. This leads to the conclusion I have already suggested (as does the NMI Report). The only way water could have entered the GAUL in sufficient quantity to destroy her ability to right herself was through an opening on the trawl deck.

It is a pity that having located the wreck and having a camera taking photos of her, the television crew were prevented from examining the openings on the trawl deck by overhanging nets from other trawlers which had previously snagged on the wreck.

The sea took the GAUL and her crew as it has taken so many trawlers in the past. It had, or needed, no help from the Russians. Since the end of the Second World War there are many cases where a British trawler and crew have vanished without trace, without sending any distress signal. On or about the 16 December

1948 the Fleetwood trawler GOTH and her 21 crew vanished off the northwest coast of Iceland. In January 1953 the Grimsby trawler SHELDON and her crew vanished between the Shetland and Faroe Islands. The Fleetwood trawler RED FALCON and her 19 man crew disappeared when bound home from Iceland in December 1959. In January 1968 two Hull trawlers, the KINGSTON PERIDOT off North Iceland, and the St. ROMANUS in the North Sea, were lost with all hands. The BLUE CRUSADER and her crew from Aberdeen, and the BOSTON PIONAIR and her crew from Lowestoft, disappeared in January and February 1965. There are many more trawler losses where we can only speculate as to the cause of the loss, but in every case there are two factors in common with the loss of the GAUL. All these lost vessels were sound and seaworthy, and equipped with modern radio transmitters but no distress call was received from them. Secondly, the weather in the area they were presumed lost was very bad. Now that the position of the wreck of the GAUL has been established without doubt, I think the Marine Safety Agency should examine it to establish the cause. We owe it to the dependants of the men who perished who have been in Limbo for 24 years. But besides humanitarian reasons, the knowledge of how this tragedy occurred would give boat builders information which could possibly prevent similar disasters in the future. After all, that was why the NMI Report was commissioned in the first place.

Technicians building the model of the "GAUL" used in the Solent experiments. Photo courtesy Grimsby Evening Telegraph.

The completed model of the "GAUL". Photo courtesy Royal Institute of Naval Architects.

The "GAUL" model flooding experiments, November 1976. Photo courtesy Marine Safety Agency.

The "GAUL" model flooding experiments, November 1976. Photos courtesy Marine Safety Agency.

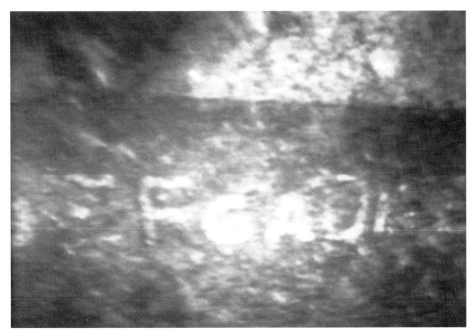

The wreck of the "GAUL" with her original name, "Ranger Castor", showing through. Photo courtesy Anglia Television Ltd.

The Bridge of the "GAUL" in her final resting place. Photo courtesy Anglia Television Ltd.

CHAPTER 11

THE PRICE OF A LIFE

Distant water trawling was a dangerous occupation, and every year trawlermen were lost. When the GAUL sank thirty-six men sank with her. Twenty-one women lost their partner and main provider, and thirty-seven children were rendered fatherless. The media gave a great deal of space to setting out the amount of compensation those bereaved families received, most of the figures being given out being incorrect or half truths. What did the dependants receive? Sadly, very little in comparison with their loss. First I will paint a broad picture and give the total amount of aid given from the various sources, then, in an appendix I will give the amounts paid to each individual.

Every Hull trawlerman was a member of the Fishermen's Pension Scheme. This insurance scheme was managed by the Hull Fishing Vessel Owners Association and the premiums were paid half by the vessel owner and half by the insured man. Under this scheme each member of the GAUL's crew received a death benefit of £2,000 with the exception of one crew member who was under the age of eighteen, and who received £1,000. Hence the total amount of the insurance money paid out to the dependants of the thirty-six men was £71,000. It was the custom in Hull that when a man was lost at sea his basic wages would be paid by the vessel's owner for thirteen weeks. The following is a copy of an internal memorandum from D.M.Oswald to Graham Hellyer dated 23 April 1974:

> D.M.Oswald   Mr.Graham Hellyer
> DMO/M.   23rd April 1974
> GAUL

"When the GAUL was presumed lost I instructed our Cashiers to continue paying the basic wage to all the dependants of the crew of the GAUL for a period of 13 weeks from the date of the loss.
This period will expire in approximately 10 days, and accordingly payment will be discontinued.
It is the H.F.V.O.A. practice to continue payment up to 13 weeks, and following the loss of the GAUL Mr. Thomas Boyd raised this point at a Management Committee Meeting at which I was not present. Mr. Boyd's suggestion was that in the case of the GAUL the period of 13 weeks should be extended to 26 weeks, but apparently his suggestion was received with no enthusiasm from any members of the Management Committee."
In the event, Tom Boyd, Managing Director of Boyd Line, got his way and wages of £28 per week were paid for twenty-six weeks, a total of £26,208.

Allowing for differentials the actual total would have been slightly more than this. Thus the combined initial payment from insurance and wages each dependant received was about £2,728.

There were two other sources of financial assistance available to dependants but payments from these funds were dependent on need. The Widows and Orphans Fund (Hull Fishermen's Trust) was set up under a trust deed in 1897, to provide relief for permanently disabled fishermen and widows and dependants of fishermen lost or killed at sea. This fund was maintained by annual contributions from the trawler owners and the crews.

At a meeting of the H.F.V.O.A. Management Committee held on 27 February 1974 the Chairman referred to the tragic loss of the GAUL and to a letter dated 20 February 1974 from the Chairman of the Trust Fund. This letter stated that as the Fund then stood it would be unable to meet the new financial commitment without the infusion of a great deal of money. The Secretary estimated that another £10,000 per annum might be required.

Those members present agreed that further capital was needed and that member companies should be asked to donate to the Fund according to the number of ships in their fleet on the following basis :- £1,500 per filleter, £1,250 per freezer, £1,000 per wet ship and £200 for each seine net vessel. It was further agreed that the present annual contribution of £100 per ship be doubled to £200, the deduction of £6 from the gross settlings of each wet fish vessel be increased to £12, and crew's contribution of 5p per week be increased to 10p per week, subject to agreement with the T.G.W.Union. As a result of the above agreement, on 16 April 1974 the H.F.V.O.A. made a "call" and British United Trawlers (Hellyer Bros. Ltd.) donated £50,000 to the Fund calculated as follows:

4 Freezers at £1,250 each	= £5,000
30 Freshers at £1,000 each	= £30,000
10 Filleters at £1,500 each	= £15,000
Total	= £50,000

A similar amount was paid into the Fund by the other Hull trawler owners.

By March 1981, over 7 years after the loss, this Fund had paid out various sums totaling £30,054.75 to 26 dependants. The largest single beneficiary was a widow with four young children who received £2,621.75 over the period. The smallest payout was a sum of £111 to a single mother. The Lord Mayor of Hull's Fishing Vessels Distress Fund was originally set up in 1955 to assist dependants of men lost at sea and was periodically renewed to run until March 1983. Renewal was dependent on the fund being financially viable. It was not exclusively for the GAUL dependants; there were other beneficiaries as well. At the time of the GAUL disaster there were substantial donations into the fund from the public (about £18,680). In the period from the loss to March 1981 the fund made payments totalling £19,064 to 18 of the GAUL's dependants. These payments ranged from £640 to a widow with no children to £1,886 to a widow with four young children. Some dependants were assessed as having "no discernible need" and consequently received no financial assistance from the above Funds. Another voluntary organisation, the Hull Round Table, set up a fund, and a cheque (amount undisclosed) is given to each child when they reach the age of 16. In August 1981 each widow and each child received a small payment to help them have a holiday.

Hull trawlermen were usually members of the Fishing Section of the Transport and General Workers Union, hence fully paid up members of the Union lost with the GAUL would have received £500 from the Union Insurance. At least one member of the GAUL's crew missed out on this.

Mr. W.J. Tracey, the man that joined the GAUL off Bridlington, completed the forms to join the Union and the authorisation for the Company to deduct and pay his Union Subscriptions. He had presumably handed the form, together with his Service Record Book, to the Shipping Master at the Company Office. He should therefore have been a fully paid up member and qualified for the £500 insurance money. However, the Company neglected to pay his union subscription as directed and the £500 was not paid to his dependants. Later investigation into the matter found the authorisation form, dated 27 March 1973, in the back of Mr Tracey's Service Book in the Shipping Office. It had never been delivered to the Cashiers. The Company declined to accept responsibility. In an internal memorandum from D.M.Oswald to G.Hellyer dated 4th April 1974 he explained ".... it turned out that the form of authorisation was in the back of Mr. Tracey's Service Book which is kept, as you know, in the Shipping Office. The standard form of practice for our Cashiers to receive a form, is that they are either sent in a batch direct from the Union Office, or the men themselves give the form to the Cashier personally. To sum up, it appears that the dependants of Mr. Tracey will not receive the £500 insurance monies although the blame for this cannot lie with the Company, the Union, or even the man himself." Now that we are in possession of all the figures we can put an average price on the life of each man that was lost. In February 1980 Mr. Laurie L.H. Swaine, Financial Director of B.U.T., set out the amounts paid out to date assuming 34 men were lost (in fact 36 men perished). My figures are slightly different.

	Re Mr. Swaine	Re. the Author
1. Insurance	£67,000	£71,000
2. Wages	£24,752	£26,208
3. Trust Fund	£30,054	£30,054
4. Lord Mayor's Fund	£19,064	£19,064
5. Out of court Set.	£16,731	£16,731
Total Payout	£157,601	£163,057
Average price per life lost:	£4,635	£4,529

In the distant water trawling industry a life certainly came cheaply. The compensation given was inadequate and by 1982 some of the dependants were described as "in great need". Hull M.P.'s John Prescott and James Johnson made strenuous efforts to persuade the owners of GAUL to provide more relief.

Correspondence between the parties lasted over three years and meetings were held with the M.P.'s and Company officials at the Associated Fisheries office in Queens Gate and at the House of Commons. All to little avail. B.U.T insisted they had done all that could be expected of them and they had met all their legal obligations. The following telex, was sent by Mr. L.H. Swaine, financial director to Mr Bill Letten, then Managing Director, and sums up the Company's attitude:

26224 AF LTD G
527044 BUTGY G
262224 AF LTD G
For the attention of Mr.W.Letten from L.H.Swaine.
28.7.82.
GAUL. FOLLOWING IS "COCKSHY".
"Thank you for your letter dated ......1982.
Whilst I appreciate that GAUL, because of the number of men lost, was an exceptional case, you will understand that, for B.U.T. to give special treatment to these dependants would create precedents which would be very unfair in comparison with the dependants of other fishermen lost at sea.

There has always been a port basis for payment of benefits to dependants, with the Hull Fishermen's Trust available to deal with cases of hardship. This fund was substantially boosted by the Hull trawler owners following the loss and in view of the likely decline in the future in the number of beneficiaries there may well be some monies which could be made available to meet specific hardship cases.

In addition, the Lord Mayor's Fund is making certain regular payments to needy dependants, and there may well be additional funds which could be released here, having regard to the possible reduction in the numbers requiring assistance following the decline in employment in the industry.

It is now eight and one half years since the GAUL was lost and I believe, therefore, that either the Lord Mayor's Fund and/or the Hull Fishermen's Trust Fund should deal with any outstanding cases of extreme hardship.

Regards."   527044 BUTGY G   262224 AF LTD G

The above telex formed the basis of a letter sent by Bill Letten to James Johnson M.P. on the 30 July 1982, and set the seal on the matter.

APPENDIX 1. Crew List of M.T.GAUL

	RATING	NAME	AGE	NEXT OF KIN
1.	Skipper	Nellist P.H	43	Mother
2.	Mate	Spurgeon M.E	37	Wife
3.	2nd Officer	Broom S	27	Wife
4.	Junior Off.	Chisholm J.M	33	Wife
5.	Radio Off.	Doone J	34	Wife
6.	Ch.Engineer	O'Brien J.R	38	Mother
7.	2nd Engineer	Bowles R	29	Parents
8.	3rd Engineer	Wales J.V	29	Wife
9.	4th Engineer	Gardner J	52	Wife
10.	Trainee Eng.	Hackett T	22	Common Law Wife
11.	Cook	Petersen N	47	Wife
12.	2nd Cook	Wheater D.A	25	Mother
13.	Ass. Cook	Straker K.J	17	Parents
14.	Factory Man.	Magee T	38	Wife
15.	Fac. Ch.Hd.	Collier S.T	40	Wife
16.	Factory Hand	Nilsson R.C	41	Wife (Divorced)
17.	" "	North T.W	26	Wife
18.	" "	Worner A.	44	Wife
19.	" "	Sheppard	54	Wife
20.	" "	Heywood J	23	Father
21.	" "	Wood H.S	53	Wife
22.	" "	Jones W.E	26	Mother
23.	" "	Atkinson R	33	Wife
24.	" "	Grundy E	42	Mother
25.	" "	McLellan J.C	18	? No dependants
26.	M. Plant Op.	Briggs C	58	Wife
27.	" " "	Smith C	46	Wife
28.	Factory Mech.	Woodhouse J.W	45	Wife
29.	Spare Hand	Clark P.E	22	Parents
30.	" "	Wilson H.W.F	27	Grand Mother
31.	" "	Chisholm	31	Wife
32.	" "	O'Brien J.W	27	Mother
33.	" "	Riley J.F	51	Wife (Divorced)
34.	" "	Dudding B	23	Parents
35.	" "	Tracey T.W	24	Father
36.	" "	Naulls C.E	32	Wife

Mate M.E. Spurgeon joined the vessel at Tromso, Norway on 28th January 1974 as a replacement for Mate G.W. Petty who sustained a rupture and was landed at Lodigen for treatment and repatriation.

Appendix 2 The Assistance Funds Payouts to February 1980

Crew Member	Dependants		Trust Fund	Mayor's Fund
1. R. Atkinson	Mrs P.A.Atkinson			
	Children	Date of Birth		
	Paul	24.06.60		
	Kevin	28.08.62		
	Andrew	22.11.63		
	Mark	22.09.65	£2,272.75	£1,559.00
	Mrs A Precious			
	Common Law Wife		£663.00	- - - -
2. C. Briggs	Wife: Mrs D.Briggs		£812.00	£640.00
3. S.J. Broom	Wife: Mrs D.I.Broom			
	Children	Date of Birth		
	Joanne	14.04.67		
	Paul	04.08.68		
	Leigh	07.11.71		
	Craig	10.10.74	£2,621.75	£1,886.00
4. R. Chisholm	C.L. Wife			
	Mrs L. Calvert		£521.50	- - - -
5. J. Chisholm	Daughter			
	Mrs S.E.Fraser		£243.00	- - - -
6. S. Collier	Wife: Mrs M.L.Collier			
	Children	Date of Birth		
	Kenneth	06.05.56		
	David	16.11.62		
	Andrew	17.05.65		
	Michael	04.04.68	£2,051.00	£1,548.00
7. J. Doone	Wife: Mrs S.Doone			
	Children	Date of Birth		
	Angela	27.06.66		
	Catherine	10.11.68		
	Martin	14.02.72	£2,108.00	£1,600.00
8. J. Gardner	Wife: Mrs E.Gardner		£812.00	£640.00
9. T. Hackett	C.L. Wife:			
	Mrs M.Page		£742.50	£622.00
	Daughter: Deborah Hackett			

Crew Member	Dependants		Trust Fund	Mayor's Fund
10. W.E. Jones	Mother: Mrs R.E. Jones		£713.25	£640.00
11. T. Magee	C.L. Wife: Miss B.L.Magee Children Date of Birth Helen Teresa 05.03.66 Gaynor Elizabeth 23.1.72 Wife:Mrs M.Magee Child: Carl Andrew 05.11.60		£1,058.75	£782.00
12. C. Naulis	Wife: Mrs J.E.Naulis Children Date of Birth Colleen 04.12.66 Kenneth 22.10.68 Julia 07.04.70		£2,202.25	£1,600.00
13. R. Nilsson	Divorced Wife: Mrs H.Nilsson Children: Graham 14.04.65 Sharon 20.02.59		£1,075.25	- - - -
14. J. North	Wife: Mrs C.A.North Children Date of Birth Carl 29.10.66 Wayne 18.05.69 Sharon 24.04.70		£2.202.25	£1,600.00
15. N. Petersen	Wife: Mrs M.Petersen Children Date of Birth Neil 27.10.57 Lynne 03.12.59		£1,777.50	- - - -
16. T. Sheppard	Wife: Mrs C.T.Sheppard		£812.00	£640.00
17. C. Smith	Wife: Mrs A.I.Smith Children Date of Birth Ian 14.09.57 Gail 18.10.63		£1,265.00	£985.00

Crew Member	Dependants	Trust Fund	Mayor's Fund
18. N. Spurgeon	Wife: Mrs S.Spurgeon Children Date of Birth Michael 04.02.60 Terence 03.06.64 Michelle 29.12.67	£1,525.00	£1,159.00
19. T. Tracey	Children Date of Birth Andrew Smith 20.2.70 Mother: Miss K.Smith	£111.00	- - - -
	Lee Morrison (6 years) Mother: Mrs Shipley formally Mrs Morrison	£208.50	- - - -
20. J. Wales	Wife: Mrs D.Wales Child Date of Birth Michelle 09.10.68	£1,244.00	£960.00
21. J. Woodhouse	Wife: Mrs L.J.Woodhouse Child Date of Birth David 27.05.63	£1,199.00	£923.00
22. H. Wilson	? Mrs Wilson	£118.00	- - - -
23. A. Worner	Wife: Mrs G.M.Worner	£847.75	£640.00
24. H. Wood	Wife: Mrs G.J.Wood	£847.75	£640.00
Total Amount paid out by the funds		£30,054.75	£19,064.00

Appendix 3
Diary of Communications from Gaul on her last voyage

Tuesday 22 January 1974
Gaul sailed from Hull on a.m. tide. Cleared the dock at 0605 GMT.

Wednesday 23 January . Reported at 1000 hours.
0900 hours position 57.50 North 02.20 East. Course 019 Speed 12 knots.

Thursday 24 January. Reported at 1000 hours.
0900 hours position 62.07 N 04.18 E. Course 027 Speed 12 knots.

Reported at 1300 hours: Cannot find following items on board: 18 Filleting Knives, 30 Aprons, 10 Baskets, 6 Wash kits, 48 Packets Soap Powder, 10 Rolls of Wire Wool, 24 Domestos, 10 Gal Disinfectant, 6 Mop Head, 6 Deck Brushes, 1 bag assorted nails. Factory Manager assures some of these are essential. Please advise.

Telegram to Gaul at 1627 hours: Most of items mentioned were placed on board. Please check further. If still required will be shipped on KELT sailing 26th.

Friday 25 January. Reported at 1000 hours.
0900 hours position 66.01 N 09.10 E Course 027 Speed 11.6 knots. Found all store items except knives, aprons, nails, plastic wash kits.
Reported at 1700 hours: Taking Mate George Petty into Lodigen, suspected rupture.

Saturday 26 January. Telephone call from Skipper Nellist at Lodigen ref. replacement Mate. Lodigen Agent reported: Gaul 0800 hours. Doctor on board for Mate George Petty - rupture - left for home 27.1.74. GAUL sailed 1600 hours 27.1.74.

Sunday 27 January. Bound Tromso to pick up replacement Mate Spurgeon. (Office informed Tromso Agent: M.E. Spurgeon left Heathrow 1730 Sunday, due Oslo 2200, due Tromso 0145 Monday 28.1.74.

Monday 28 January. Reported at 0830 hours.
9 a.m. position 70.30 N 20.55 E Course 030 Speed 11.6 knots.
Tromso Agent reported: GAUL arrived 0130 hours 28.1.74. Mate Spurgeon joined vessel. Sailed 0230 hours.

Tuesday 29 January. Reported via CASSIO on group freezer report at 0915 hours : Commenced 71.50 N 29.10 E.

Wednesday 30 January. Reported via ORSINO on group freezer report at 0900 hours: Steamed to 71.30 N 34.30 E.

Thursday 31 January. Reported at 1000 hours: Fishing same position - 71.30 N 34.30 E .

Friday 1 February. Reported via CASSIO on group freezer report at 0915 hours: Position 71.25 N 34.35 E.

Saturday 2 February. Reported via PICT on group freezer report at 1000 hours: Same position - 71.25 N 34.25 E.

Sunday 3 February. Reported via CASSIO on group freezer report at 0915 hours: Fishing at Harbakken.

Monday 4 February. Reported 0900 hours: Total on board 10 tons. Fishing at Harbakken.

Tuesday 5 February. Reported via ARAB on group freezer report.

Wednesday 6 February. Reported via PICT on group freezer report at 0920 hours: Fishing North Cape Bank.

Thursday 7 February. Reported at 1000 hours: Fishing 72.15 N 24.50 E. Also made link-call to Hull office reporting a Sperry fault to the Superintendent Engineer.

Friday 8 February. Reported via PICT on group freezer report at 0930 hours: Laid and dodging North Cape Bank.
At 1030 hours she reported to ORSINO on the Skippers Freezer Schedule. Between 11.06 and 11.09 she sent two private telegrams by radio through Wick Radio.
GAUL was never heard on the radio again.

Saturday 9 February. No report received.

Sunday 10 February. No report received. "Spy" message sent to GAUL from the office at 1200 hours.

Monday 11 February. Message sent from office at 1320 hours GMT to ARAB, DANE, CASSIO, KELT, ORSINO and PICT: "You should proceed to implement search for Gaul at last known position 72.15 N 24.50 E.

12, 13, 14 February. Group search operation for GAUL.

Friday 15 February. Group search operation terminated p.m. GAUL presumed lost.

BIBLIOGRAPHY

1. Minutes of Proceedings of the Board of Trade Formal Investigation into the Loss of the MT GAUL.

2 Lloyd's Register.

3. National Maritime Institute Report on Project 207001

4. Loss of M.T. GAUL. Evidence of Second Defendants By G.Donaldson / Brooke Marine.

5. The Gaul Disaster: An Investigation into the Loss of a Large Stern Trawler. by A.Morrall.

6. Y-Yard Report/2424/78 Y.1603 Further Investigation into the technical aspects of the loss of M.T.Gaul.

Profile of the Author

John Nicklin, a native of Fleetwood, came from a fishing family and made his first trips to sea at the age of ten, using his school holidays to do pleasure trips with his father, John "Shonners" Nicklin in the ST Dinamar and his great uncle, Bill "Slippy" Wright, in the ST Fane. He started a deep sea fishing career at the age of 16 during the war, signing on the ST Strathblair as brassie. Five years later found him a fully fledged decky in one of the top Fleetwood trawlers, the Red Knight with Skipper Eric Littler.

In 1947 he moved with his family to Grimsby and started work with Northern Trawlers (later British United Trawlers) as decky on Northern Dawn, followed two years on Northern Duke with Bill Woods, a year on Northern Gem with Jimmy Latham and five years on Northern Pride. He did his first trip as Skipper on the Pride in 1954. In addition to his time in the Northern Boats he served as Mate on the Lincoln City, Real Madrid, Derby County, Everton and Grimsby Town owned by Consolidated Fisheries.

In 1969 he moved to Ghana and commanded the Factory Stern Trawlers Mamla and Kamba, and finishing as Operations/Production Manager of the State Fishing Corporation. Returning to the UK in 1974 he joined the Merchant Navy as Chief Navigating Officer and worked on Hydrographic Survey Vessels until he retired in 1986. During his time in the M.N. he took a B.A. degree majoring in mathematics. After retirement he was a voluntary maths tutor with the Adult Education Service before working part time as a tutor with Maritime Open Learning teaching Maritime Law and Shipmasters Business. At the age of 72 he is still active working with the National Sea Training Centre, and is currently tutoring over 50 prospective Masters and Skippers for their MSA Certificates. His previous writing includes *Trawling with the Lid Off,* several text books for candidates for Masters and Skippers Certificates, a training course for tug masters for Forth Tugs which was made compulsory reading for all masters in the company, and articles on shipping and fishing. He has done consultancy work in the training field for the Seafish Industry Authority and has written the text books and compiled the courses for the new NVQs at levels 3 and 4 in Marine Law for North West Kent College.